Singapore MATH PRACTICE

LEVEL 1B

Appropriate for Students in GRADE 2

Thinking Kids®
An imprint of Carson-Dellosa Publishing LLC
Greensboro, North Carolina

W9-BAP-308

Visit carsondellosa.com for correlations to Common Core, state, national, and Canadian provincial standards.

ISBN 978-0-7682-4001-6
11-146207784

INTRODUCTION TO SINGAPORE MATH

Welcome to Singapore Math! The math curriculum in Singapore has been recognized worldwide for its excellence in producing students highly skilled in mathematics. Students in Singapore have ranked at the top in the world in mathematics on the *Trends in International Mathematics and Science Study* (TIMSS) in 1993, 1995, 2003, and 2008. Because of this, Singapore Math has gained in interest and popularity in the United States.

Singapore Math curriculum aims to help students develop the necessary math concepts and process skills for everyday life and to provide students with the ability to formulate, apply, and solve problems. Mathematics in the Singapore Primary (Elementary) Curriculum cover fewer topics but in greater depth. Key math concepts are introduced and built-on to reinforce various mathematical ideas and thinking. Students in Singapore are typically one grade level ahead of students in the United States.

The following pages provide examples of the various math problem types and skill sets taught in Singapore.

At an elementary level, some simple mathematical skills can help students understand mathematical principles. These skills are the counting-on, counting-back, and crossing-out methods. Note that these methods are most useful when the numbers are small.

1. The Counting-On Method

Used for addition of two numbers. Count on in 1s with the help of a picture or number line.

$$7 + 4 = \mathbf{11}$$

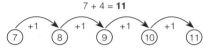

2. The Counting-Back Method

Used for subtraction of two numbers. Count back in 1s with the help of a picture or number line.

$$16 - 3 = \mathbf{13}$$

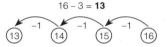

3. The Crossing-Out Method

Used for subtraction of two numbers. Cross out the number of items to be taken away. Count the remaining ones to find the answer.

$$20 - 12 = \mathbf{8}$$

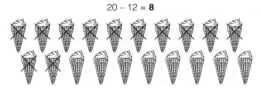

A **number bond** shows the relationship in a simple addition or subtraction problem. The number bond is based on the concept "part-part-whole." This concept is useful in teaching simple addition and subtraction to young children.

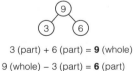

To find a whole, students must add the two parts.
To find a part, students must subtract the other part from the whole.

The different types of number bonds are illustrated below.

1. Number Bond (single digits)

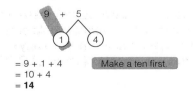

$$3 \text{ (part)} + 6 \text{ (part)} = \mathbf{9} \text{ (whole)}$$
$$9 \text{ (whole)} - 3 \text{ (part)} = \mathbf{6} \text{ (part)}$$
$$9 \text{ (whole)} - 6 \text{ (part)} = \mathbf{3} \text{ (part)}$$

2. Addition Number Bond (single digits)

$$= 9 + 1 + 4 \qquad \boxed{\text{Make a ten first.}}$$
$$= 10 + 4$$
$$= \mathbf{14}$$

3. Addition Number Bond (double and single digits)

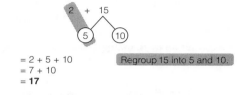

$$= 2 + 5 + 10 \qquad \boxed{\text{Regroup 15 into 5 and 10.}}$$
$$= 7 + 10$$
$$= \mathbf{17}$$

4. Subtraction Number Bond (double and single digits)

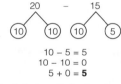

$$10 - 7 = 3$$
$$3 + 2 = \mathbf{5}$$

5. Subtraction Number Bond (double digits)

$$10 - 5 = 5$$
$$10 - 10 = 0$$
$$5 + 0 = \mathbf{5}$$

Students should understand that multiplication is repeated addition and that division is the grouping of all items into equal sets.

1. Repeated Addition (Multiplication)

Mackenzie eats 2 rolls a day. How many rolls does she eat in 5 days?

$$2 + 2 + 2 + 2 + 2 = 10$$
$$5 \times 2 = 10$$

She eats **10** rolls in 5 days.

2. The Grouping Method (Division)

Mrs. Lee makes 14 sandwiches. She gives all the sandwiches equally to 7 friends. How many sandwiches does each friend receive?

$$14 \div 7 = 2$$

Each friend receives **2** sandwiches.

One of the basic but essential math skills students should acquire is to perform the 4 operations of whole numbers and fractions. Each of these methods is illustrated below.

1. The Adding-Without-Regrouping Method

```
  H  T  O
  3  2  1          O: Ones
+ 5  6  8          T: Tens
---------          H: Hundreds
  8  8  9
```

Since no regrouping is required, add the digits in each place value accordingly.

2. The Adding-by-Regrouping Method

```
   H  T  O
  ¹4  9  2          O: Ones
+  1  5  3          T: Tens
-----------         H: Hundreds
   6  4  5
```

In this example, regroup 14 tens into 1 hundred 4 tens.

3. The Adding-by-Regrouping-Twice Method

```
      H  T  O
     ¹2 ¹8 6
   +   3  6  5
   ─────────────
      6  5  1
```

O: Ones
T: Tens
H: Hundreds

Regroup twice in this example.
First, regroup 11 ones into 1 ten 1 one.
Second, regroup 15 tens into 1 hundred 5 tens.

4. The Subtracting-Without-Regrouping Method

```
      H  T  O
      7  3  9
   -  3  2  5
   ─────────────
      4  1  4
```

O: Ones
T: Tens
H: Hundreds

Since no regrouping is required, subtract the digits in each place value accordingly.

5. The Subtracting-by-Regrouping Method

```
      H  T  O
      5  ⁷8 ¹¹1
   -  2  4  7
   ─────────────
      3  3  4
```

O: Ones
T: Tens
H: Hundreds

In this example, students cannot subtract 7 ones from 1 one. So, regroup the tens and ones. Regroup 8 tens 1 one into 7 tens 11 ones.

6. The Subtracting-by-Regrouping-Twice Method

```
      H  T  O
     ⁷8 ⁹0 ¹⁰0
   -  5  9  3
   ─────────────
      2  0  7
```

O: Ones
T: Tens
H: Hundreds

In this example, students cannot subtract 3 ones from 0 ones and 9 tens from 0 tens. So, regroup the hundreds, tens, and ones. Regroup 8 hundreds into 7 hundreds 9 tens 10 ones.

7. The Multiplying-Without-Regrouping Method

```
      T  O
      2  4
   ×     2
   ─────────
      4  8
```

O: Ones
T: Tens

Since no regrouping is required, multiply the digit in each place value by the multiplier accordingly.

8. The Multiplying-With-Regrouping Method

```
      H  T  O
     ¹3 ²4 9
   ×        3
   ─────────────
   1, 0  4  7
```

O: Ones
T: Tens
H: Hundreds

In this example, regroup 27 ones into 2 tens 7 ones, and 14 tens into 1 hundred 4 tens.

9. The Dividing-Without-Regrouping Method

```
         2  4  1
      ┌───────────
    2 │ 4  8  2
      │-4
      │────
      │   8
      │  -8
      │  ────
      │      2
      │     -2
      │     ───
      │      0
```

Since no regrouping is required, divide the digit in each place value by the divisor accordingly.

10. The Dividing-With-Regrouping Method

```
         1  6  6
      ┌───────────
    5 │ 8  3  0
      │-5
      │────
      │  3  3
      │ -3  0
      │ ─────
      │     3  0
      │    -3  0
      │    ─────
      │        0
```

In this example, regroup 3 hundreds into 30 tens and add 3 tens to make 33 tens. Regroup 3 tens into 30 ones.

11. The Addition-of-Fractions Method

$$\frac{1}{6} \times \frac{2}{2} + \frac{1}{4} \times \frac{3}{3} = \frac{2}{12} + \frac{3}{12} = \mathbf{\frac{5}{12}}$$

Always remember to make the denominators common before adding the fractions.

12. The Subtraction-of-Fractions Method

$$\frac{1}{2} \times \frac{5}{5} - \frac{1}{5} \times \frac{2}{2} = \frac{5}{10} - \frac{2}{10} = \mathbf{\frac{3}{10}}$$

Always remembers to make the denominators common before subtracting the fractions.

13. The Multiplication-of-Fractions Method

$$\frac{^1\cancel{3}}{5} \times \frac{1}{_3\cancel{9}} = \mathbf{\frac{1}{15}}$$

When the numerator and the denominator have a common multiple, reduce them to their lowest fractions.

14. The Division-of-Fractions Method

$$\frac{7}{9} \div \frac{1}{6} = \frac{7}{_3\cancel{9}} \times \frac{\cancel{6}^2}{1} = \frac{14}{3} = \mathbf{4\frac{2}{3}}$$

When dividing fractions, first change the division sign (÷) to the multiplication sign (×). Then, switch the numerator and denominator of the fraction on the right hand side. Multiply the fractions in the usual way.

Model drawing is an effective strategy used to solve math word problems. It is a visual representation of the information in word problems using bar units. By drawing the models, students will know of the variables given in the problem, the variables to find, and even the methods used to solve the problem.

Drawing models is also a versatile strategy. It can be applied to simple word problems involving addition, subtraction, multiplication, and division. It can also be applied to word problems related to fractions, decimals, percentage, and ratio.

The use of models also trains students to think in an algebraic manner, which uses symbols for representation.

The different types of bar models used to solve word problems are illustrated below.

1. The model that involves addition

Melissa has 50 blue beads and 20 red beads. How many beads does she have altogether?

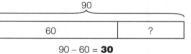

$50 + 20 = \mathbf{70}$

2. The model that involves subtraction

Ben and Andy have 90 toy cars. Andy has 60 toy cars. How many toy cars does Ben have?

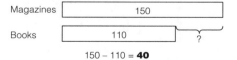

$90 - 60 = \mathbf{30}$

3. The model that involves comparison

Mr. Simons has 150 magazines and 110 books in his study. How many more magazines than books does he have?

Magazines	150	
Books	110	?

$150 - 110 = \mathbf{40}$

4. The model that involves two items with a difference

A pair of shoes costs $109. A leather bag costs $241 more than the pair of shoes. How much is the leather bag?

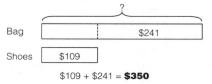

$109 + $241 = **$350**

Singapore Math Practice Level 1B

5. The model that involves multiples

Mrs. Drew buys 12 apples. She buys 3 times as many oranges as apples. She also buys 3 times as many cherries as oranges. How many pieces of fruit does she buy altogether?

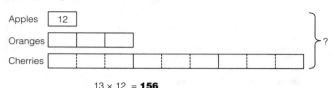

$$13 \times 12 = \textbf{156}$$

6. The model that involves multiples and difference

There are 15 students in Class A. There are 5 more students in Class B than in Class A. There are 3 times as many students in Class C than in Class A. How many students are there altogether in the three classes?

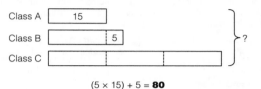

$$(5 \times 15) + 5 = \textbf{80}$$

7. The model that involves creating a whole

Ellen, Giselle, and Brenda bake 111 muffins. Giselle bakes twice as many muffins as Brenda. Ellen bakes 9 fewer muffins than Giselle. How many muffins does Ellen bake?

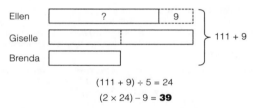

$$(111 + 9) \div 5 = 24$$
$$(2 \times 24) - 9 = \textbf{39}$$

8. The model that involves sharing

There are 183 tennis balls in Basket A and 97 tennis balls in Basket B. How many tennis balls must be transferred from Basket A to Basket B so that both baskets contain the same number of tennis balls?

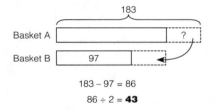

$$183 - 97 = 86$$
$$86 \div 2 = \textbf{43}$$

9. The model that involves fractions

George had 355 marbles. He lost $\frac{1}{5}$ of the marbles and gave $\frac{1}{4}$ of the remaining marbles to his brother. How many marbles did he have left?

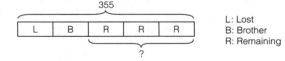

L: Lost
B: Brother
R: Remaining

5 parts → 355 marbles
1 part → 355 ÷ 5 = 71 marbles
3 parts → 3 × 71 = **213** marbles

10. The model that involves ratio

Aaron buys a tie and a belt. The prices of the tie and belt are in the ratio 2 : 5. If both items cost $539,

(a) what is the price of the tie?

(b) what is the price of the belt?

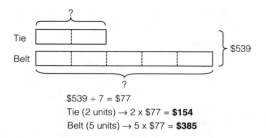

$539 ÷ 7 = $77
Tie (2 units) → 2 × $77 = **$154**
Belt (5 units) → 5 × $77 = **$385**

11. The model that involves comparison of fractions

Jack's height is $\frac{2}{3}$ of Leslie's height. Leslie's height is $\frac{3}{4}$ of Lindsay's height. If Lindsay is 160 cm tall, find Jack's height and Leslie's height.

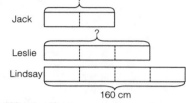

1 unit → 160 ÷ 4 = 40 cm

Leslie's height (3 units) → 3 × 40 = **120 cm**

Jack's height (2 units) → 2 × 40 = **80 cm**

Thinking skills and strategies are important in mathematical problem solving. These skills are applied when students think through the math problems to solve them. Below are some commonly used thinking skills and strategies applied in mathematical problem solving.

1. Comparing

Comparing is a form of thinking skill that students can apply to identify similarities and differences.

When comparing numbers, look carefully at each digit before deciding if a number is greater or less than the other. Students might also use a number line for comparison when there are more numbers.

Example:

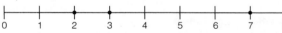

3 is greater than 2 but smaller than 7.

2. Sequencing

A sequence shows the order of a series of numbers. *Sequencing* is a form of thinking skill that requires students to place numbers in a particular order. There are many terms in a sequence. The terms refer to the numbers in a sequence.

To place numbers in a correct order, students must first find a rule that generates the sequence. In a simple math sequence, students can either add or subtract to find the unknown terms in the sequence.

Example: Find the 7th term in the sequence below.

1,	4,	7,	10,	13,	16	?
1st term	2nd term	3rd term	4th term	5th term	6th term	7th term

Step 1: This sequence is in an increasing order.

Step 2: 4 − 1 = 3   7 − 4 = 3
The difference between two consecutive terms is 3.

Step 3: 16 + 3 = 19
The 7th term is **19**.

3. Visualization

Visualization is a problem solving strategy that can help students visualize a problem through the use of physical objects. Students will play a more active role in solving the problem by manipulating these objects.

The main advantage of using this strategy is the mobility of information in the process of solving the problem. When students make a wrong step in the process, they can retrace the step without erasing or canceling it.

The other advantage is that this strategy helps develop a better understanding of the problem or solution through visual objects or images. In this way, students will be better able to remember how to solve these types of problems.

Some of the commonly used objects for this strategy are toothpicks, straws, cards, strings, water, sand, pencils, paper, and dice.

4. Look for a Pattern

This strategy requires the use of observational and analytical skills. Students have to observe the given data to find a pattern in order to solve the problem. Math word problems that involve the use of this strategy usually have repeated numbers or patterns.

Example: Find the sum of all the numbers from 1 to 100.

Step 1: Simplify the problem.
Find the sum of 1, 2, 3, 4, 5, 6, 7, 8, 9, and 10.

Step 2: Look for a pattern.

$1 + 10 = 11$ $2 + 9 = 11$ $3 + 8 = 11$
$4 + 7 = 11$ $5 + 6 = 11$

Step 3: Describe the pattern.
When finding the sum of 1 to 10, add the first and last numbers to get a result of 11. Then, add the second and second last numbers to get the same result. The pattern continues until all the numbers from 1 to 10 are added. There will be 5 pairs of such results. Since each addition equals 11, the answer is then $5 \times 11 = 55$.

Step 4: Use the pattern to find the answer.
Since there are 5 pairs in the sum of 1 to 10, there should be ($10 \times 5 = 50$ pairs) in the sum of 1 to 100.
Note that the addition for each pair is not equal to 11 now. The addition for each pair is now ($1 + 100 = 101$).

$50 \times 101 = 5050$

The sum of all the numbers from 1 to 100 is **5,050**.

5. Working Backward

The strategy of working backward applies only to a specific type of math word problem. These word problems state the end result, and students are required to find the total number. In order to solve these word problems, students have to work backward by thinking through the correct sequence of events. The strategy of working backward allows students to use their logical reasoning and sequencing to find the answers.

Example: Sarah has a piece of ribbon. She cuts the ribbon into 4 equal parts. Each part is then cut into 3 smaller equal parts. If the length of each small part is 35 cm, how long is the piece of ribbon?

$3 \times 35 = 105$ cm
$4 \times 105 = 420$ cm

The piece of ribbon is **420 cm**.

6. The Before-After Concept

The *Before-After* concept lists all the relevant data before and after an event. Students can then compare the differences and eventually solve the problems. Usually, the Before-After concept and the mathematical model go hand in hand to solve math word problems. Note that the Before-After concept can be applied only to a certain type of math word problem, which trains students to think sequentially.

Example: Kelly has 4 times as much money as Joey. After Kelly uses some money to buy a tennis racquet, and Joey uses $30 to buy a pair of pants, Kelly has twice as much money as Joey. If Joey has $98 in the beginning,
(a) how much money does Kelly have in the end?
(b) how much money does Kelly spend on the tennis racquet?

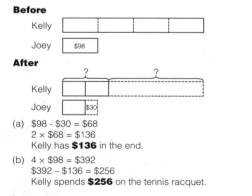

Before

Kelly

Joey $98

After

Kelly

Joey $30

(a) $98 - $30 = $68
$2 \times $68 = 136
Kelly has **$136** in the end.

(b) $4 \times $98 = 392
$392 - $136 = 256
Kelly spends **$256** on the tennis racquet.

7. Making Supposition

Making supposition is commonly known as "making an assumption." Students can use this strategy to solve certain types of math word problems. Making assumptions will eliminate some possibilities and simplifies the word problems by providing a boundary of values to work within.

Example: Mrs. Jackson bought 100 pieces of candy for all the students in her class. How many pieces of candy would each student receive if there were 25 students in her class?

In the above word problem, assume that each student received the same number of pieces. This eliminates the possibilities that some students would receive more than others due to good behaviour, better results, or any other reason.

8. Representation of Problem

In problem solving, students often use representations in the solutions to show their understanding of the problems. Using representations also allow students to understand the mathematical concepts and relationships as well as to manipulate the information presented in the problems. Examples of representations are diagrams and lists or tables.

Diagrams allow students to consolidate or organize the information given in the problems. By drawing a diagram, students can see the problem clearly and solve it effectively.

A list or table can help students organize information that is useful for analysis. After analyzing, students can then see a pattern, which can be used to solve the problem.

9. Guess and Check

One of the most important and effective problem-solving techniques is *Guess and Check*. It is also known as *Trial and Error*. As the name suggests, students have to guess the answer to a problem and check if that guess is correct. If the guess is wrong, students will make another guess. This will continue until the guess is correct.

It is beneficial to keep a record of all the guesses and checks in a table. In addition, a *Comments* column can be included. This will enable students to analyze their guess (if it is too high or too low) and improve on the next guess. Be careful; this problem-solving technique can be tiresome without systematic or logical guesses.

Example: Jessica had 15 coins. Some of them were 10-cent coins and the rest were 5-cent coins. The total amount added up to $1.25. How many coins of each kind were there?

Use the guess-and-check method.

Number of 10¢ Coins	Value	Number of 5¢ Coins	Value	Total Number of Coins	Total Value
7	$7 \times 10¢ = 70¢$	8	$8 \times 5¢ = 40¢$	$7 + 8 = 15$	$70¢ + 40¢ = 110¢$ $= 1.10
8	$8 \times 10¢ = 80¢$	7	$7 \times 5¢ = 35¢$	$8 + 7 = 15$	$80¢ + 35¢ = 115¢$ $= 1.15
10	$10 \times 10¢ = 100¢$	5	$5 \times 5¢ = 25¢$	$10 + 5 = 15$	$100¢ + 25¢ = 125¢$ $= 1.25

There were **ten** 10-cent coins and **five** 5-cent coins.

10. Restate the Problem

When solving challenging math problems, conventional methods may not be workable. Instead, restating the problem will enable students to see some challenging problems in a different light so that they can better understand them.

The strategy of restating the problem is to "say" the problem in a different and clearer way. However, students have to ensure that the main idea of the problem is not altered.

How do students restate a math problem?

First, read and understand the problem. Gather the given facts and unknowns. Note any condition(s) that have to be satisfied.

Next, restate the problem. Imagine narrating this problem to a friend. Present the given facts, unknown(s), and condition(s). Students may want to write the "revised" problem. Once the "revised" problem is analyzed, students should be able to think of an appropriate strategy to solve it.

11. Simplify the Problem

One of the commonly used strategies in mathematical problem solving is simplification of the problem. When a problem is simplified, it can be "broken down" into two or more smaller parts. Students can then solve the parts systematically to get to the final answer.

Table of Contents

Singapore Math Practice Level 1B

8

LEARNING OUTCOMES

Unit 10 Mass
Students should be able to
- find the mass of objects in units.
- compare and arrange the mass of objects.
- understand the words *light*, *lighter*, *lightest*, *heavy*, *heavier*, and *heaviest*.

Unit 11 Picture Graphs
Students should be able to
- create picture graphs based on the given data.
- understand and interpret data from picture graphs.

Review 1
This review tests students' understanding of Units 10 & 11.

Unit 12 Numbers 1-40
Students should be able to
- recognize numbers up to 40.
- group numbers into tens and ones.
- compare numbers up to 40.
- arrange numbers in order up to 40.
- complete number patterns.
- add and subtract numbers up to 40.
- add 3 numbers.
- solve addition and subtraction story problems.

Unit 13 Mental Calculations
Students should be able to
- add 2 numbers without regrouping mentally.
- subtract 2 numbers without regrouping mentally.

Unit 14 Multiplying
Students should be able to
- write correct multiplication sentences.
- find the total in multiplication sentences.
- solve 1-step multiplication story problems.

Review 2
This review tests students' understanding of Units 12, 13, & 14.

Unit 15 Dividing
Students should be able to
- find the number of items in each group.
- find the number of groups.

Unit 16 Time
Students should be able to
- read time at the hour and half hour.

Review 3
This review tests students' understanding of Units 15 & 16.

Unit 17 Numbers 1-100
Students should be able to
- recognize numbers up to 100.
- group numbers into tens and ones.
- compare numbers up to 100.
- complete number patterns.
- add and subtract numbers up to 100.
- solve 1-step story problems.

Unit 18 Money (Part 1)
Students should be able to
- count coins and bills in different denominations.
- match money of one denomination to the same value of another denomination.

Unit 19 Money (Part 2)
Students should be able to
- perform addition and subtraction in dollars.
- perform addition and subtraction in cents.
- solve story problems related to money.

Review 4
This review tests students' understanding of Units 17, 18, & 19.

Final Review
This review is an excellent assessment of students' understanding of all the topics in this book.

Singapore Math Practice Level 1B

FORMULA SHEET

Unit 10 Mass

Comparing the mass of 2 objects

When 2 objects of different masses are placed on a balance, the object that sinks is heavier.

When 2 objects of different masses are placed on a balance, the object that rises is lighter.

When both sides of the balance are equal in height, the objects have the same mass.

To find the mass of an object, look at the number of units needed to balance the mass of the object.

Unit 11 Picture Graphs

To create a picture graph,
- collect data.
- organize and place the data in a table.

You can read and use the picture graph to answer questions.

Note that the symbol used in the picture graph stands for 1 item.

Unit 12 Numbers 1-40

Numerals	Words	Numerals	Words
21	twenty-one	31	thirty-one
22	twenty-two	32	thirty-two
23	twenty-three	33	thirty-three
24	twenty-four	34	thirty-four
25	twenty-five	35	thirty-five
26	twenty-six	36	thirty-six
27	twenty-seven	37	thirty-seven
28	twenty-eight	38	thirty-eight
29	twenty-nine	39	thirty-nine
30	thirty	40	forty

Place value

Numbers greater than 10 can be grouped into tens and ones.

Example:

35 = **3** tens **5** ones

Number patterns

When completing number patterns,
- see if the number pattern is in an increasing or a decreasing order.
- observe the difference between each number.
- add or subtract to get the next number.

Number order

When arranging numbers in order, determine if the series starts with the smallest or the largest number.

Comparing numbers

The words *greater than* and *more than* mean addition (+).

The words *smaller than* and *less than* mean subtraction (–).

The word *is* means equal to (=).

Example:

_____ is 3 more than 19.

_____ = 3 + 19

Adding numbers
- Add the digits in the ones place first.
- If the answer is more than 9, regroup the ones and carry a one to the tens place.
- Add the digits in the tens place. Remember to add the one that was carried if there is one.

Subtracting numbers
- Subtract the digits in the ones place first.
- If subtraction is not possible in the ones place, regroup the tens and lend a ten (10) to the ones.
- Subtract the digits in the ones place.
- Then, subtract the digits in the tens place.

Adding 3 numbers
- Make a ten first.
- Add the remaining numbers to get a sum.
- Add the ten to the sum to get the final answer.

Unit 13 Mental Calculations

Adding a 2-digit number and a 1-digit number mentally

Singapore Math Practice Level 1B

- Regroup the 2-digit number into tens and ones.
- Add the ones to get a sum.
- Add the sum to the tens to get the final answer.

Adding a 2-digit number and tens mentally
- Regroup the 2-digit number into tens and ones.
- Add the tens to get a sum.
- Add the ones to the sum to get the final answer.

Subtracting a 1-digit number from a 2-digit number mentally
- Regroup the 2-digit number into tens and ones.
- Subtract the ones.
- Add the ones to the tens to get the final answer.

Subtracting tens from a 2-digit number mentally
- Regroup the 2-digit number into tens and ones.
- Subtract the tens to get the result.
- Add the result to the ones to get the final answer.

Unit 14 Multiplication
Multiplication is repeated addition.

The sign $\times$ is used to represent multiplication in a number sentence.

Example:
$$4 + 4 + 4 = 12$$
$$3 \times 4 = 12$$

Unit 15 Division
Division is the opposite of multiplication.

Division allows us to find the equal number of items in each group. It also allows us to find the number of groups.

Unit 16 Time
There are 2 hands on the face of a clock.
The short hand is called the *hour hand*. The long hand is called the *minute hand*.

Numbers 1 to 12 are displayed on the face of the clock.
There are 24 hours in a day, so the hour and minute hands go around twice every day.

When the hour hand is at 2 and the minute hand is at 12, the time is read as 2 o'clock.

When the hour hand is between 2 and 3 and the minute hand is at 6, the time is read as 2:30.

Unit 17 Numbers 1-100

Numerals	Words
50	fifty
60	sixty
70	seventy
80	eighty
90	ninety
100	one hundred

Adding a 2-digit number and a 2-digit number
- Add the digits in the ones place. If the sum is more than 10, regroup the ones and carry a one to the tens place.
- Add the digits in the tens place. Add the one that was carried if there is one.

Subtracting a 2-digit number from a 2-digit number
- Subtract the digits in the ones place. If it is not possible, regroup the tens and lend a ten (10) to the ones.
- Subtract the digits in the tens place accordingly.

Unit 18 Money (Part 1)
The symbol for cents is ¢.
The symbol for dollars is $.

Ways of exchanging coins
1 ten-cent coin = 2 five-cent coins
1 twenty-five cent coin = 5 five-cent coins
    = 25 one-cent coins
1 fifty-cent coin = 5 ten-cent coins
1 dollar coin = 10 ten-cent coins
    = 4 twenty-five-cent coins
    = 2 fifty-cent coins

Ways of exchanging bills
1 one-dollar bill = 1 one-dollar coin
1 ten-dollar bill = 10 one-dollar coins
    = 2 five-dollar bills

Unit 19 Money (Part 2)
Adding in cents or in dollars
1. Add the digits in the ones place. If the sum is more than 10, carry a one to the tens place.
2. Add the digits in the tens place. Add the one that was carried if there is one.

Subtracting in cents or in dollars
1. Subtract the digits in the ones place. If this is not possible, lend a ten (10) to the ones.
2. Subtract the digits in the tens place.

Singapore Math Practice Level 1B

12

Unit 10: MASS

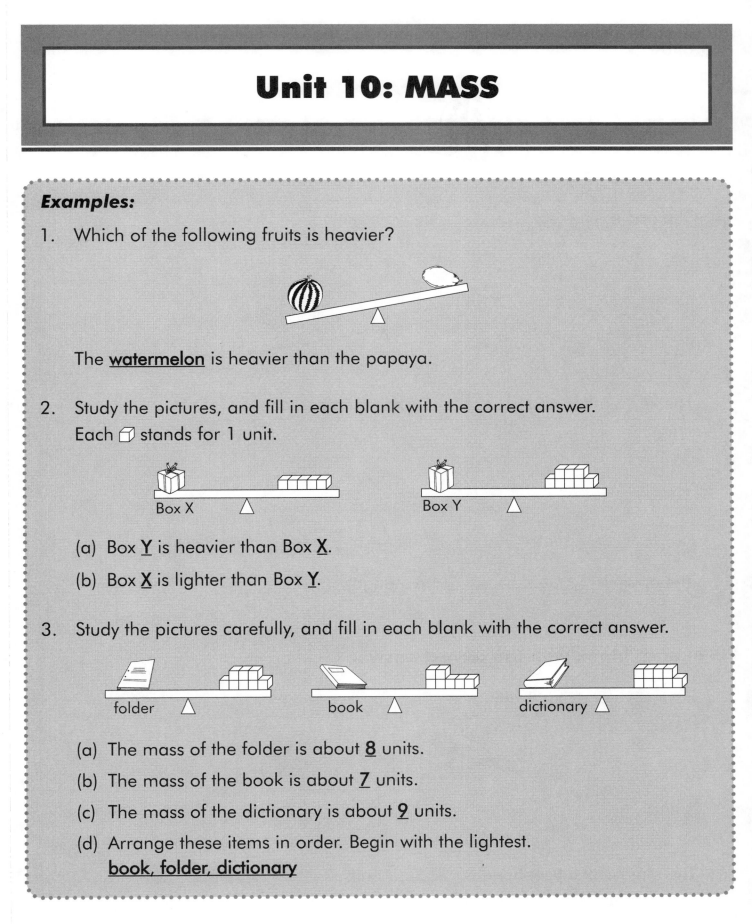

Examples:

1. Which of the following fruits is heavier?

    The **watermelon** is heavier than the papaya.

2. Study the pictures, and fill in each blank with the correct answer.
    Each ▢ stands for 1 unit.

    Box X

    Box Y

    (a) Box **Y** is heavier than Box **X**.

    (b) Box **X** is lighter than Box **Y**.

3. Study the pictures carefully, and fill in each blank with the correct answer.

    folder   book   dictionary

    (a) The mass of the folder is about **8** units.

    (b) The mass of the book is about **7** units.

    (c) The mass of the dictionary is about **9** units.

    (d) Arrange these items in order. Begin with the lightest.
         book, folder, dictionary

13

Singapore Math Practice Level 1B

Fill in each blank with as heavy as, heavier than, **or** lighter than.

1.

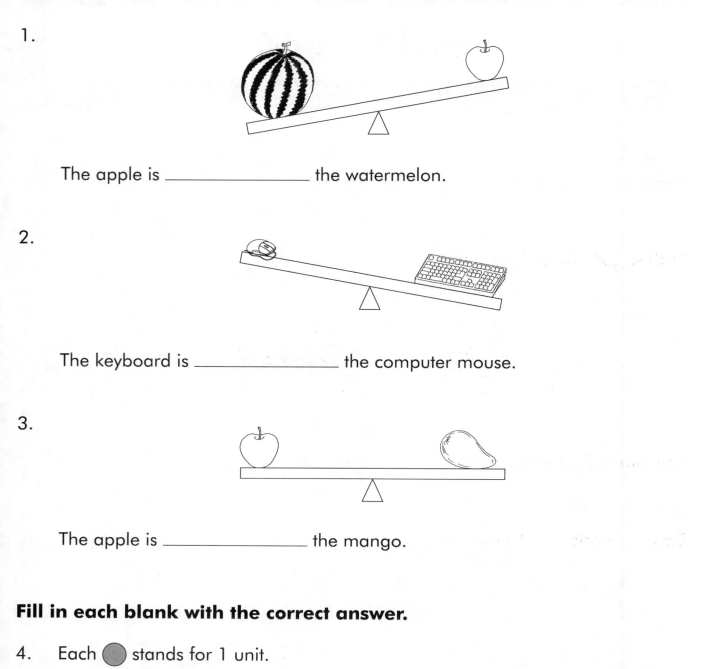

The apple is _____ the watermelon.

2.

The keyboard is _____ the computer mouse.

3.

The apple is _____ the mango.

Fill in each blank with the correct answer.

4. Each ⬤ stands for 1 unit.

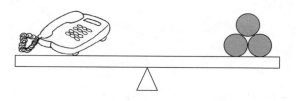

The mass of the telephone is _____ units.

Singapore Math Practice Level 1B

5. Each ▨ stands for 1 unit.

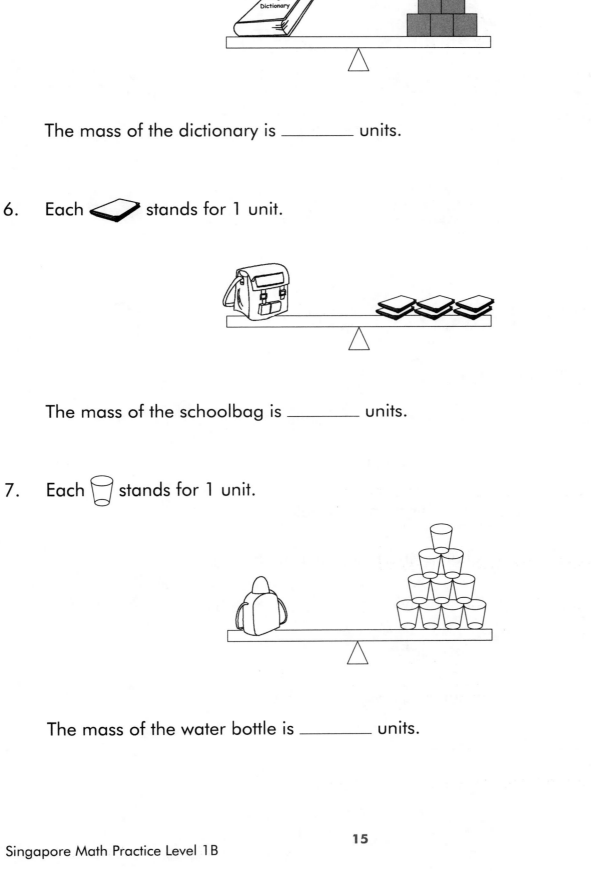

   The mass of the dictionary is _____ units.

6. Each ▱ stands for 1 unit.

   The mass of the schoolbag is _____ units.

7. Each ▽ stands for 1 unit.

   The mass of the water bottle is _____ units.

Singapore Math Practice Level 1B

Fill in each blank with the correct answer.

Each 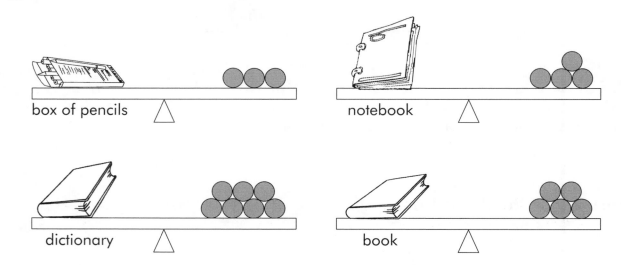 stands for 1 unit.

8. The mass of the notebook is _____ units.

9. The mass of the dictionary is _____ units.

10. The mass of the box of pencils is _____ units.

11. The mass of the book is _____ units.

12. The _____ is heavier than the book.

13. The _____ is lighter than the notebook.

14. The _____ is the heaviest.

15. The _____ is the lightest.

16. Arrange the 4 items in order. Begin with the lightest.

_____, _____, _____, _____
lightest

Singapore Math Practice Level 1B

Fill in each blank with the correct answer.

Each 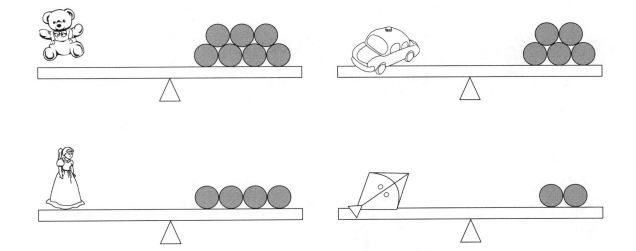 stands for 1 unit.

17. The mass of the teddy bear is _____ units.

18. The mass of the toy car is _____ units.

19. The mass of the doll is _____ units.

20. The mass of the kite is _____ units.

21. The doll is heavier than the _____.

22. The toy car is lighter than the _____.

23. The _____ is the lightest.

24. The _____ is the heaviest.

25. The _____ is lighter than the toy car but heavier than the kite.

Singapore Math Practice Level 1B

Fill in each blank with the correct answer.

Each 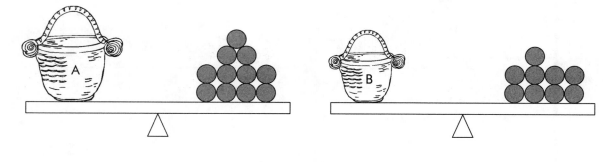 stands for 1 unit.

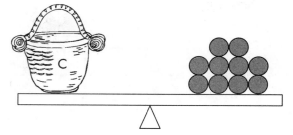

26. The mass of Basket A is _____ units.

27. The mass of Basket B is _____ units.

28. The mass of Basket C is _____ units.

29. Basket _____ is lighter than Basket C.

30. Basket _____ is heavier than Basket C.

31. Basket _____ is the heaviest.

32. Basket _____ is the lightest.

33. Arrange the baskets in order. Begin with the heaviest.

_____, _____, _____
    heaviest

Fill in each blank with the correct answer.

Each 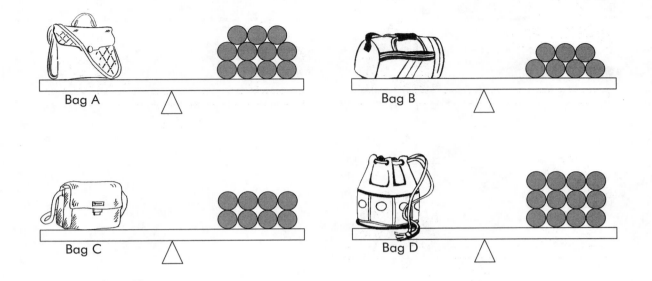 stands for 1 unit.

34. Bag _____ is the heaviest.

35. Bag _____ is the lightest.

36. The mass of Bag A is _____ units.

37. The mass of Bag D is _____ units.

38. Bag C is heavier than Bag _____.

39. Bag _____ is heavier than Bag C but lighter than Bag D.

40. Arrange the 4 bags in order. Begin with the heaviest.

   _____, _____, _____, _____
   heaviest

Unit 11: PICTURE GRAPHS

Examples:

This graph shows the number of stickers collected by a group of children in a week.

Each ◯ stands for 1 sticker.

(a)   How many stickers did Eduardo collect?   <u>6</u>

(b)   How many stickers did Kelly collect?   <u>9</u>

(c)   How many more stickers did Eduardo collect than Nick?   <u>2</u>

(d)   How many fewer stickers did Nick collect than Kelly?   <u>5</u>

(e)   Who collected the most stickers?   <u>Kelly</u>

(f)   Who collected the fewest stickers?   <u>Nick</u>

(g)   How many stickers did the children collect in a week?

$7 + 6 + 4 + 9 = \underline{26}$

1. Anna went to the zoo last Sunday. Study the picture carefully. Draw a picture graph of the animals she saw in the zoo. Use  to stand for 1 animal.

Monkeys	
Lions	
Tigers	
Giraffes	
Parrots	

Singapore Math Practice Level 1B

2. Study the picture carefully. Draw a picture graph of the games the children are playing. Use ⭐ to stand for 1 child.

Hopscotch	Soccer	Jumping Rope	Marbles

Singapore Math Practice Level 1B

3. The picture below shows a group of children at the park. Study the picture carefully. Draw a picture graph of the activities the children are doing. Use  to stand for 1 child.

Soccer	
Kite-Flying	
Feeding Ducks	
Walking	

Singapore Math Practice Level 1B

The graph below shows food Mrs. Lee sells at her restaurant. Study the graph carefully. Fill in each blank with the correct answer.

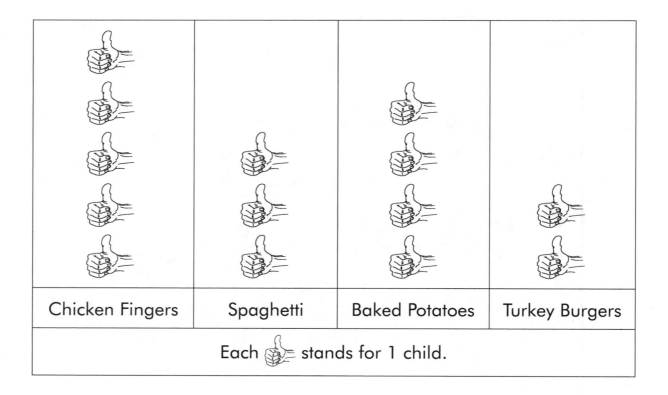

4. _____ children buy baked potatoes.

5. _____ children buy chicken fingers.

6. The least popular food is the _____.

7. The most popular food is the _____.

8. _____ more children buy baked potatoes than turkey burgers.

9. _____ fewer children buy spaghetti than chicken fingers.

This graph shows the favorite sports of the students in a class. Study the graph carefully. Fill in each blank with the correct answer.

Basketball	👦👦👦👦👦👦👦
Swimming	👦👦👦👦👦👦
Football	👦👦👦👦👦👦👦👦👦👦
Baseball	👦👦👦👦👦👦
Karate	👦👦👦👦

Each 👦 stands for 1 student.

10. _____ students like baseball.

11. _____ students like football.

12. The most popular sport is _____.

13. The least popular sport is _____.

14. The number of students who like _____ and

    _____ is the same.

15. _____ more students like basketball than karate.

16. _____ fewer students like karate than football.

17. There are _____ students in the class altogether.

Singapore Math Practice Level 1B

The graph below shows the types of insects in a school garden. Study the graph carefully. Fill in each blank with the correct answer.

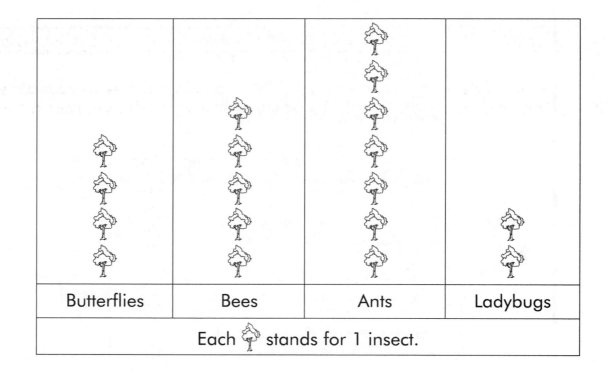

18. There are _____ butterflies.

19. There are _____ ladybugs.

20. There are more _____ than other insects.

21. There are fewer _____ than other insects.

22. There are _____ fewer butterflies than ants.

23. There are _____ more bees than ladybugs.

24. There are _____ insects altogether.

Singapore Math Practice Level 1B

REVIEW 1

The picture graph below shows the number of cups of water each container can hold. Study the graph carefully. Fill in each blank with the correct answer.

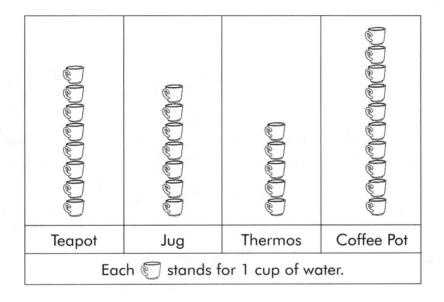

Each 🍵 stands for 1 cup of water.

1. The teapot can hold _____ cups of water.

2. The thermos can hold _____ cups of water.

3. The container that can hold the fewest cups of water is the _____.

4. The container that can hold the most cups of water is the _____.

5. The teapot can hold _____ more cups of water than the thermos.

6. The jug can hold _____ fewer cups of water than the coffee pot.

Fill in each blank with the correct answer.

Each 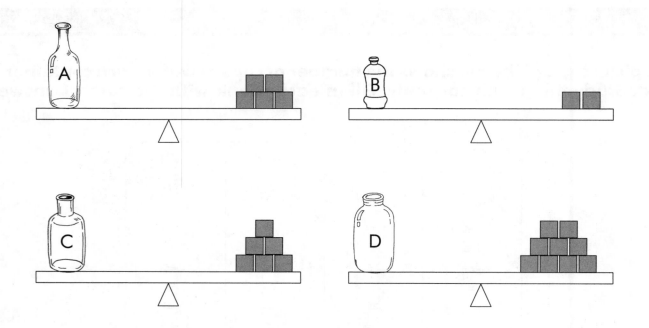 stands for 1 unit.

7. The mass of Bottle A is _____ units.

8. The mass of Bottle B is _____ units.

9. The mass of Bottle C is _____ units.

10. The mass of Bottle D is _____ units.

11. Bottle _____ is the heaviest.

12. Bottle _____ is the lightest.

Singapore Math Practice Level 1B

13. The picture below shows a class of students at a park. Study the picture carefully. Draw a picture graph of the activities the students are doing.

Kite-Flying	Riding Bikes	Feeding Birds	Walking
Each ⭐ stands for 1 student.			

Fill in each blank with heavier than, lighter than, **or** as heavy as.

14.

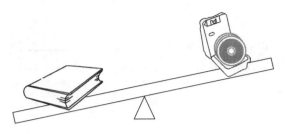

The book is _____ the CDs.

15.

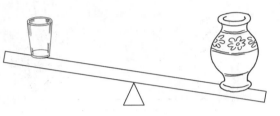

The glass is _____ the vase.

16.

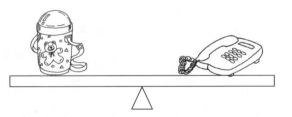

The water bottle is _____ the telephone.

17.

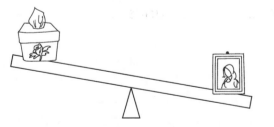

The picture frame is _____ the box of tissues.

Study the pictures below. Fill in each blank with the correct answer.

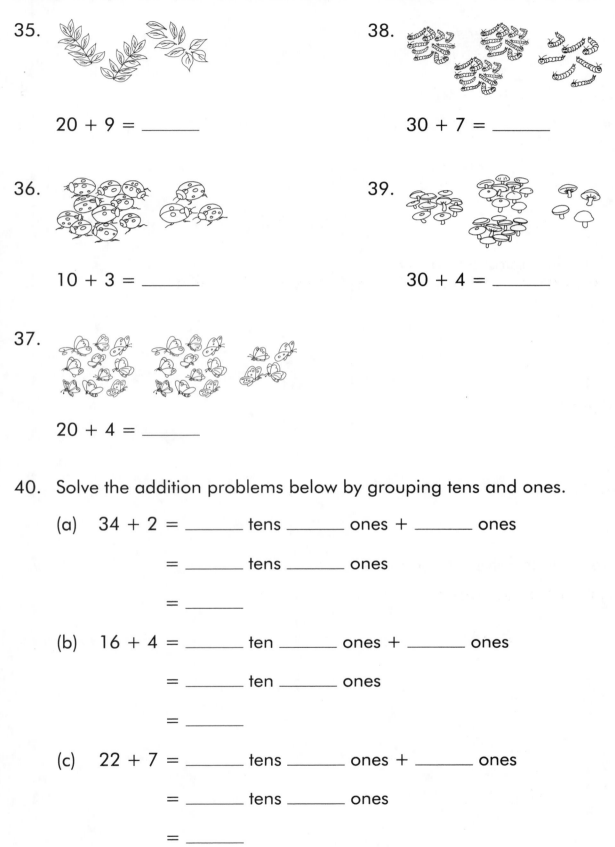

35.

20 + 9 = _____

38.

30 + 7 = _____

36.

10 + 3 = _____

39.

30 + 4 = _____

37.

20 + 4 = _____

40. Solve the addition problems below by grouping tens and ones.

(a) 34 + 2 = _____ tens _____ ones + _____ ones

= _____ tens _____ ones

= _____

(b) 16 + 4 = _____ ten _____ ones + _____ ones

= _____ ten _____ ones

= _____

(c) 22 + 7 = _____ tens _____ ones + _____ ones

= _____ tens _____ ones

= _____

Singapore Math Practice Level 1B

(d) 24 + 8 = _____ tens _____ ones + _____ ones

= _____ tens _____ ones

= _____

(e) 27 + 7 = _____ tens _____ ones + _____ ones

= _____ tens _____ ones

= _____

41. Solve each addition problem below.

(a)
```
  1 3
+ 1 3
```

(d)
```
  1 1
+ 2 6
```

(b)
```
  2 4
+ 1 5
```

(e)
```
  3 0
+   6
```

(c)
```
  3 5
+   2
```

42. Add and regroup to solve the problems.

(a)
```
  2 9
+   7
```

(d)
```
  1 9
+ 1 6
```

(b)
```
  1 5
+ 1 8
```

(e)
```
  2 5
+   6
```

(c)
```
  2 8
+ 1 2
```

Singapore Math Practice Level 1B

43. Match each child to the correct house.

44. Fill in each blank with the correct answer.

(a)

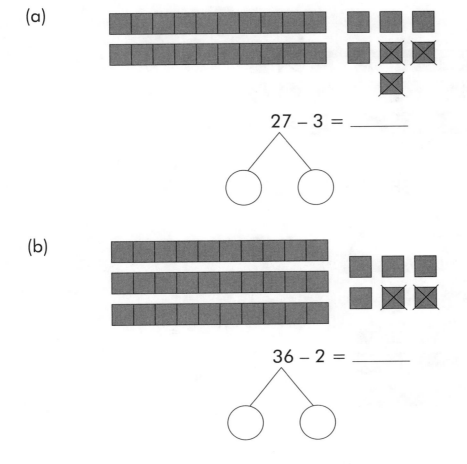

$27 - 3 =$ _____

(b)

$36 - 2 =$ _____

Singapore Math Practice Level 1B

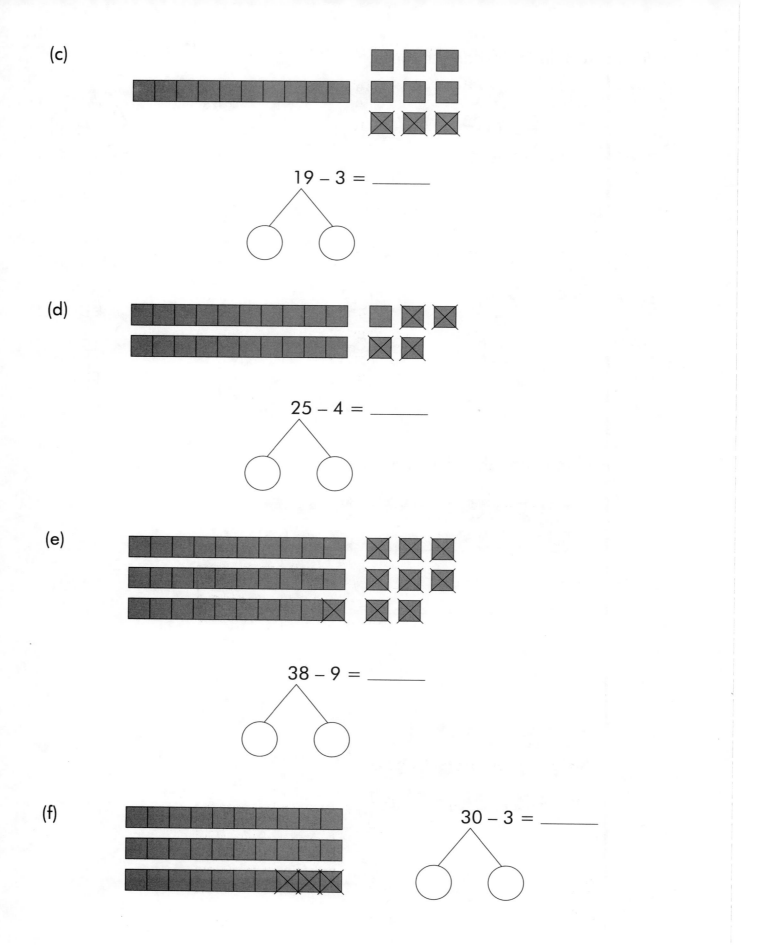

(c)

$19 - 3 =$ _____

(d)

$25 - 4 =$ _____

(e)

$38 - 9 =$ _____

(f)

$30 - 3 =$ _____

45. Solve the subtraction problems below by grouping tens and ones.

(a) 26 – 2 = _____ tens _____ ones – _____ ones

= _____ tens _____ ones

= _____

(b) 37 – 3 = _____ tens _____ ones – _____ ones

= _____ tens _____ ones

= _____

(c) 16 – 1 = _____ ten _____ ones – _____ one

= _____ ten _____ ones

= _____

(d) 24 – 4 = _____ tens _____ ones – _____ ones

= _____ tens _____ ones

= _____

(e) 33 – 4 = _____ tens _____ ones – _____ ones

= _____ tens _____ ones – _____ ones

= _____ tens _____ ones

= _____

46. Solve each subtraction problem below.

(a)
$$\begin{array}{r} 28 \\ -7 \\ \hline \end{array}$$

(c)
$$\begin{array}{r} 19 \\ -6 \\ \hline \end{array}$$

(e)
$$\begin{array}{r} 37 \\ -13 \\ \hline \end{array}$$

(b)
$$\begin{array}{r} 35 \\ -12 \\ \hline \end{array}$$

(d)
$$\begin{array}{r} 25 \\ -11 \\ \hline \end{array}$$

Singapore Math Practice Level 1B

47. Subtract by regrouping tens and ones.

(a)   3 2
      – 1 8
      _____

(c)   2 6
      – 1 7
      _____

(e)   3 0
      –   9
      _____

(b)   4 0
      – 1 5
      _____

(d)   2 3
      – 1 4
      _____

48. Match each child to the correct house.

Fill in each blank with the correct answer.

49. 3 + 5 + 7 = _____

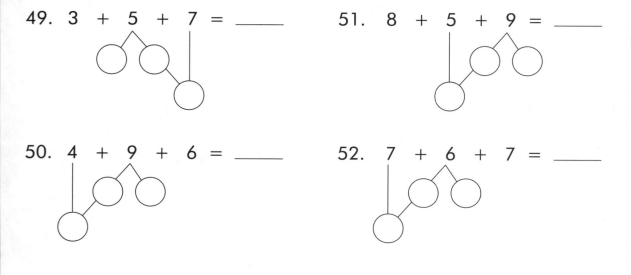

51. 8 + 5 + 9 = _____

50. 4 + 9 + 6 = _____

52. 7 + 6 + 7 = _____

Singapore Math Practice Level 1B

Add the three numbers in each problem. Write the correct answer on the line.

53. 8 + 6 + 3 = _____   55. 8 + 7 + 6 = _____

54. 9 + 4 + 5 = _____   56. 9 + 6 + 8 = _____

57. Solve the problems listed below. Write your answers in words in the crossword puzzle.

Across

1.   13 – 5

3.   8 – 3

4.   6 + 6

5.   12 – 9

6.   10 + 5

7.   18 – 9

Down

1.   7 + 4

2.   20 – 3

3.   17 – 13

5.   11 + 9

Singapore Math Practice Level 1B

Solve the story problems below. Show your work in the space.

58. Tomás has 21 bookmarks. His mother gives him another 9 bookmarks. How many bookmarks does he have now?

    He has _____ bookmarks now.

59. Charlotte has 35 stickers. She gives 19 stickers to her sister. How many stickers does she have left in the end?

    She has _____ stickers left in the end.

60. Uncle Donald has 26 eggs on his farm. Uncle Jack has 8 fewer eggs than Uncle Donald. How many eggs does Uncle Jack have?

    Uncle Jack has _____ eggs.

61. Zoe has 16 pencils. Parker has 14 pencils more than Zoe. How many pencils does Parker have?

    Parker has _____ pencils.

Singapore Math Practice Level 1B

Unit 13: MENTAL CALCULATIONS

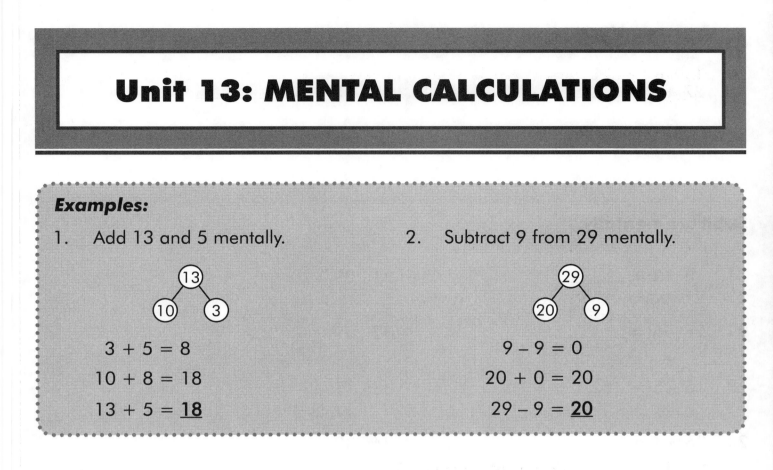

Examples:

1. Add 13 and 5 mentally.

$3 + 5 = 8$

$10 + 8 = 18$

$13 + 5 = \underline{\textbf{18}}$

2. Subtract 9 from 29 mentally.

$9 - 9 = 0$

$20 + 0 = 20$

$29 - 9 = \underline{\textbf{20}}$

Add mentally.

1. $3 + 12 =$ _____

2. $2 + 17 =$ _____

3. $11 + 5 =$ _____

4. $25 + 4 =$ _____

5. $17 + 10 =$ _____

6. $22 + 7 =$ _____

7. $32 + 6 =$ _____

8. $29 + 10 =$ _____

9. $8 + 30 =$ _____

10. $14 + 3 =$ _____

11. $6 + 20 =$ _____

12. $15 + 3 =$ _____

13. $21 + 6 =$ _____

14. $33 + 4 =$ _____

Singapore Math Practice Level 1B

15. $10 + 9 =$ _____

16. $27 + 2 =$ _____

17. $16 + 10 =$ _____

18. $7 + 11 =$ _____

19. $13 + 6 =$ _____

20. $20 + 2 =$ _____

Subtract mentally.

21. $18 - 3 =$ _____

22. $28 - 6 =$ _____

23. $15 - 5 =$ _____

24. $36 - 4 =$ _____

25. $14 - 10 =$ _____

26. $33 - 2 =$ _____

27. $16 - 3 =$ _____

28. $19 - 5 =$ _____

29. $24 - 4 =$ _____

30. $33 - 30 =$ _____

31. $39 - 20 =$ _____

32. $29 - 4 =$ _____

33. $17 - 2 =$ _____

34. $39 - 3 =$ _____

35. $23 - 2 =$ _____

36. $14 - 3 =$ _____

37. $28 - 10 =$ _____

38. $35 - 4 =$ _____

39. $37 - 10 =$ _____

40. $25 - 3 =$ _____

Unit 14: MULTIPLYING

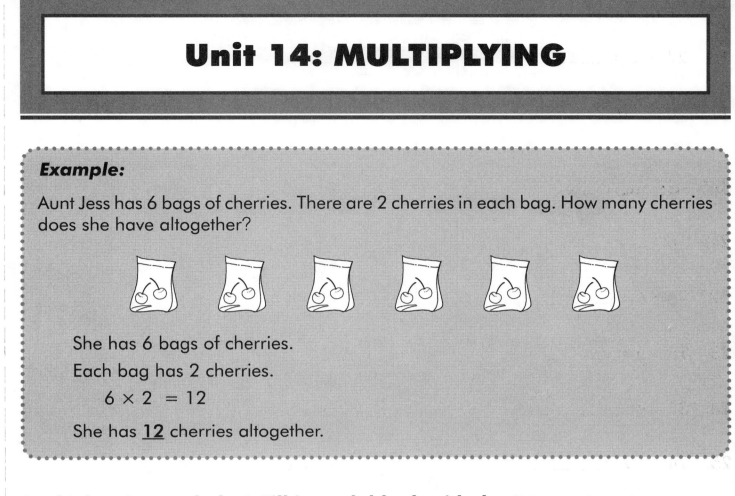

Example:

Aunt Jess has 6 bags of cherries. There are 2 cherries in each bag. How many cherries does she have altogether?

She has 6 bags of cherries.

Each bag has 2 cherries.

$6 \times 2 = 12$

She has **12** cherries altogether.

Study the pictures below. Fill in each blank with the correct answer.

1.

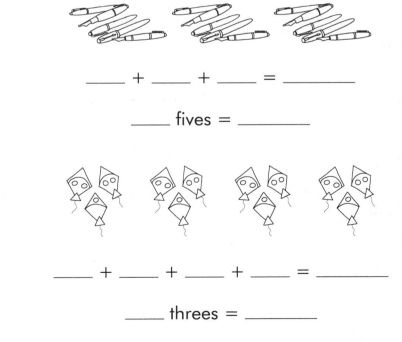

___ + ___ + ___ = _____

___ fives = _____

2.

___ + ___ + ___ + ___ = _____

___ threes = _____

Singapore Math Practice Level 1B

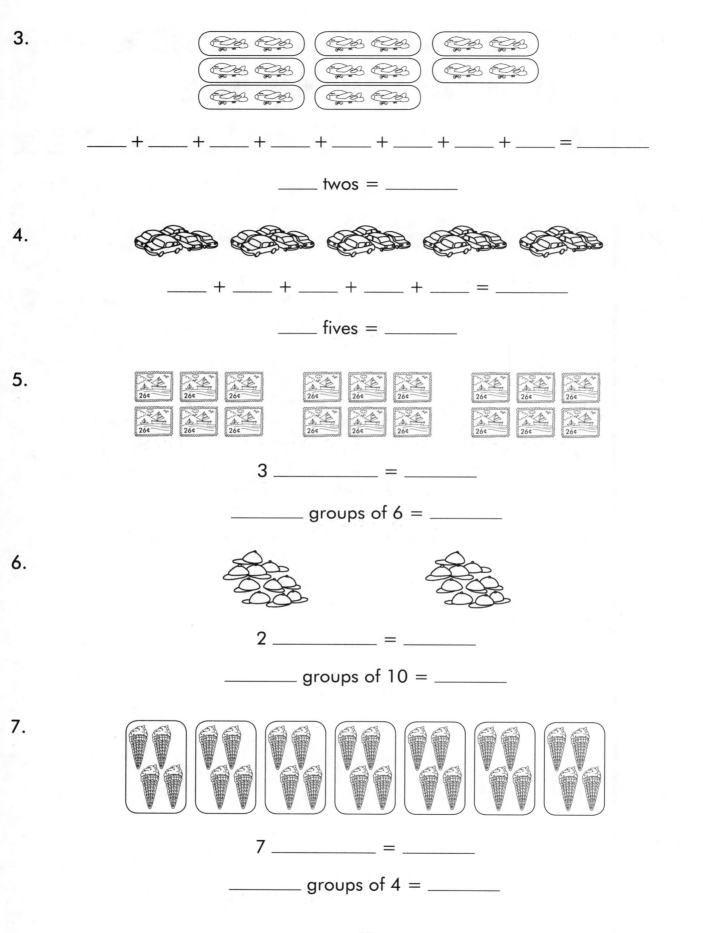

3.

____ + ____ + ____ + ____ + ____ + ____ + ____ + ____ = _____

____ twos = _____

4.

____ + ____ + ____ + ____ + ____ = _____

____ fives = _____

5.

3 _____ = _____

_____ groups of 6 = _____

6.

2 _____ = _____

_____ groups of 10 = _____

7.

7 _____ = _____

_____ groups of 4 = _____

Singapore Math Practice Level 1B

8.

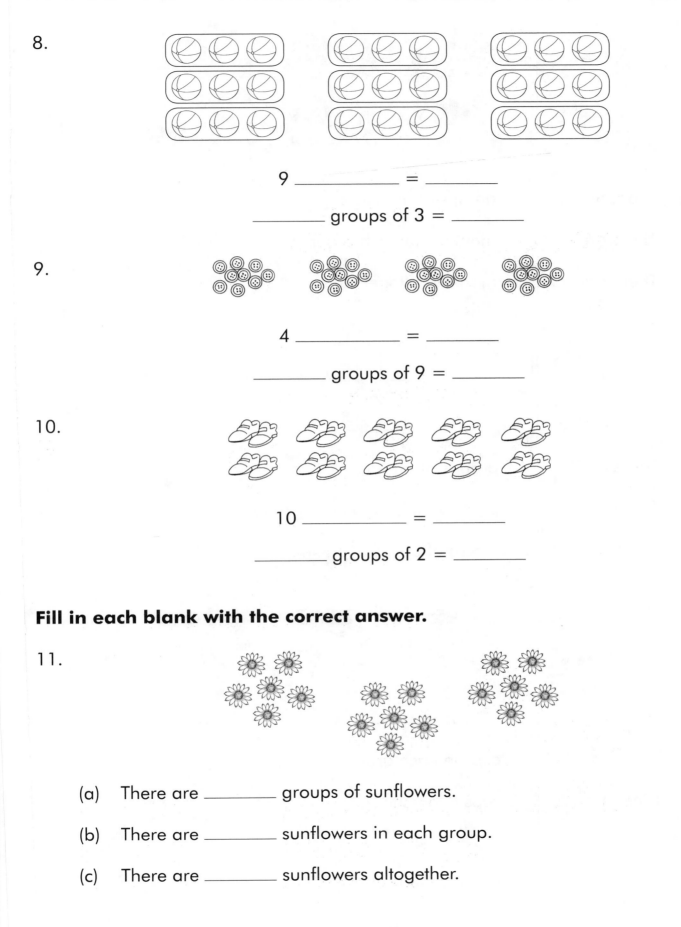

9 _____ = _____

_____ groups of 3 = _____

9.

4 _____ = _____

_____ groups of 9 = _____

10.

10 _____ = _____

_____ groups of 2 = _____

Fill in each blank with the correct answer.

11.

(a)   There are _____ groups of sunflowers.

(b)   There are _____ sunflowers in each group.

(c)   There are _____ sunflowers altogether.

Singapore Math Practice Level 1B

12.

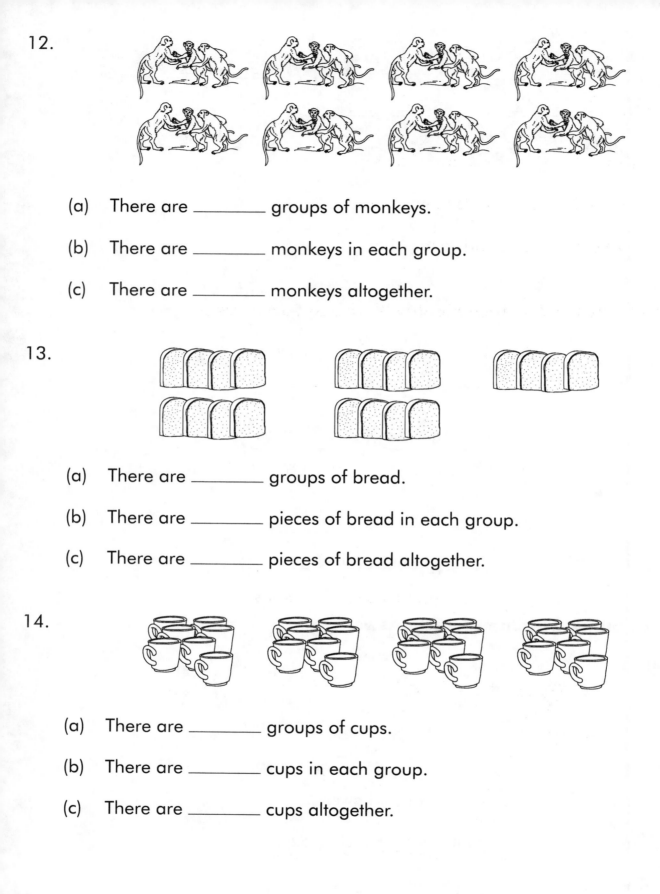

(a)   There are _____ groups of monkeys.

(b)   There are _____ monkeys in each group.

(c)   There are _____ monkeys altogether.

13.

(a)   There are _____ groups of bread.

(b)   There are _____ pieces of bread in each group.

(c)   There are _____ pieces of bread altogether.

14.

(a)   There are _____ groups of cups.

(b)   There are _____ cups in each group.

(c)   There are _____ cups altogether.

Singapore Math Practice Level 1B

15.

(a) There are _____ groups of girls.

(b) There are _____ girls in each group.

(c) There are _____ girls altogether.

Study the pictures. Fill in each blank with the correct answer.

16.

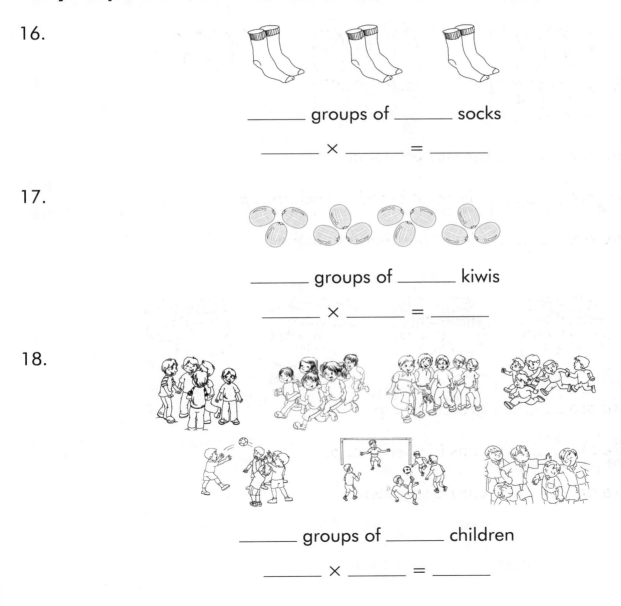

_____ groups of _____ socks

_____ × _____ = _____

17.

_____ groups of _____ kiwis

_____ × _____ = _____

18.

_____ groups of _____ children

_____ × _____ = _____

Singapore Math Practice Level 1B

19.

_____ groups of _____ watches

_____ × _____ = _____

20.

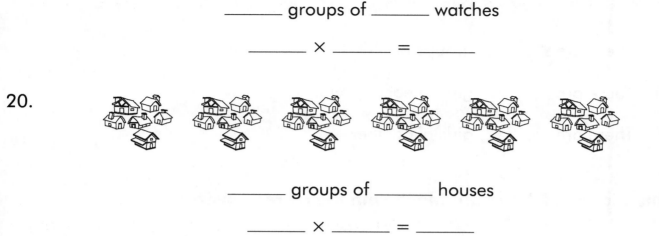

_____ groups of _____ houses

_____ × _____ = _____

Solve the following story problems.

21.

There are 4 vases. There are 5 flowers in each vase. How many flowers are there altogether?

_____ × _____ = _____

There are _____ flowers altogether.

22.

There are 8 baskets. There are 3 pieces of fruit in each basket. How many pieces of fruit are there altogether?

_____ × _____ = _____

There are _____ pieces of fruit altogether.

Singapore Math Practice Level 1B

23.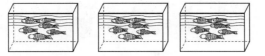

There are 3 fish tanks in a shop. There are 6 fish in each tank. How many fish are there altogether?

_____ × _____ = _____

There are _____ fish altogether.

24.

There are 8 horses on a farm. Each horse has 4 legs. How many legs does the group of horses have altogether?

_____ × _____ = _____

The group of horses has _____ legs altogether.

25.

Kimiko has 5 flags. There are 3 stars on each flag. How many stars are there altogether?

_____ × _____ = _____

There are _____ stars altogether.

26.

There are 4 plates on the table. There are 5 pieces of cake on each plate. How many pieces of cake are there altogether?

_____ × _____ = _____

There are _____ pieces of cake altogether.

Singapore Math Practice Level 1B

27.

Jamila has 9 pairs of earrings. Each pair has 2 earrings. How many earrings does Jamila have altogether?

_____ × _____ = _____

Jamila has _____ earrings altogether.

28.

There are 4 trees in a garden. Liam sees 7 birds on each tree. How many birds does Liam see altogether?

_____ × _____ = _____

Liam sees _____ birds altogether.

29.

There are 3 groups of boys on a field. There are 4 boys in each group. How many boys are there altogether?

_____ × _____ = _____

There are _____ boys altogether.

30.

Beatriz has 2 bags of lollipops. There are 8 lollipops in each bag. How many lollipops does Beatriz have altogether?

_____ × _____ = _____

Beatriz has _____ lollipops altogether.

Singapore Math Practice Level 1B

REVIEW 2

1. Write the numbers on the lines.

    (a) twelve _____

    (b) twenty-eight _____

    (c) thirty-five _____

    (d) eleven _____

    (e) sixteen _____

2. Write the following numbers in words.

    (a) 40 _____

    (b) 29 _____

    (c) 13 _____

    (d) 38 _____

    (e) 15 _____

Fill in each blank with the correct answer.

3. 5 less than 20 is _____.

4. 1 more than 39 is _____.

5. 3 less than 27 is _____.

6. 4 more than 15 is _____.

7. 2 less than 17 is _____.

Study the pictures. Fill in each blank with the correct answer.

8.

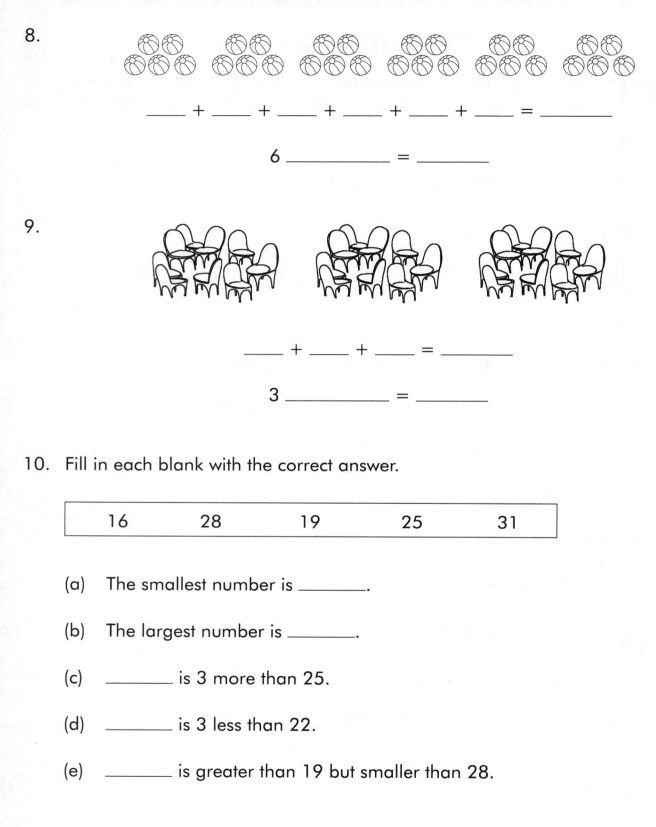

_____ + _____ + _____ + _____ + _____ + _____ = _____

6 _____ = _____

9.

_____ + _____ + _____ = _____

3 _____ = _____

10. Fill in each blank with the correct answer.

16	28	19	25	31

(a) The smallest number is _____.

(b) The largest number is _____.

(c) _____ is 3 more than 25.

(d) _____ is 3 less than 22.

(e) _____ is greater than 19 but smaller than 28.

Singapore Math Practice Level 1B

11. Solve the following problems by grouping tens and ones.

(a) 36 – 6 = _____ tens _____ ones – _____ ones

= _____ tens _____ ones

= _____

(b) 27 – 9 = _____ tens _____ ones – _____ ones

= _____ ten _____ ones – _____ ones

= _____ ten _____ ones

= _____

(c) 16 – 7 = _____ ten _____ ones – _____ ones

= _____ ten _____ ones – _____ ones

= _____ tens _____ ones

= _____

12. Complete the number patterns.

(a) _____, 12, 16, 20, _____

(b) _____, _____, 25, 28, 31

13. Solve each addition problem below.

(a)   1 2
   + 2 4
  ————

(c)   2 5
   +   6
  ————

(b)   1 5
   + 1 3
  ————

(d)   1 9
   + 1 7
  ————

57

14. Solve each subtraction problem below.

(a)
```
    1 9
 -    8
 _____
```

(c)
```
    4 0
 -  1 5
 _____
```

(b)
```
    2 7
 -  1 4
 _____
```

(d)
```
    3 5
 -  1 9
 _____
```

15. Add 31 and 7 mentally. _____

16. Subtract 10 from 28 mentally. _____

17. 5 + 8 + 4 = _____

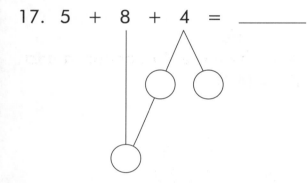

Solve the following story problems. Show your work.

18. George has 24 seashells. He gives 8 shells to his best friend. How many shells does George have left?

George has _____ seashells left.

Singapore Math Practice Level 1B

19. Mom bought 3 bags of crackers. There were 7 packages of crackers in each bag. How many packages of crackers were there altogether?

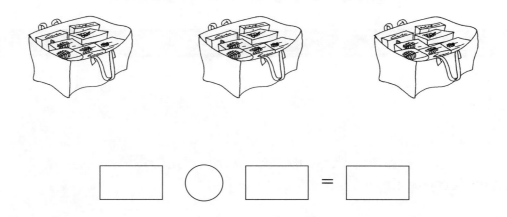

$$\boxed{} \bigcirc \boxed{} = \boxed{}$$

There were _____ packages of crackers altogether.

20. Madeline buys 8 bunches of bananas in a market. There are 4 bananas in each bunch. How many bananas are there altogether?

$$\boxed{} \bigcirc \boxed{} = \boxed{}$$

There are _____ bananas altogether.

Unit 15: DIVIDING

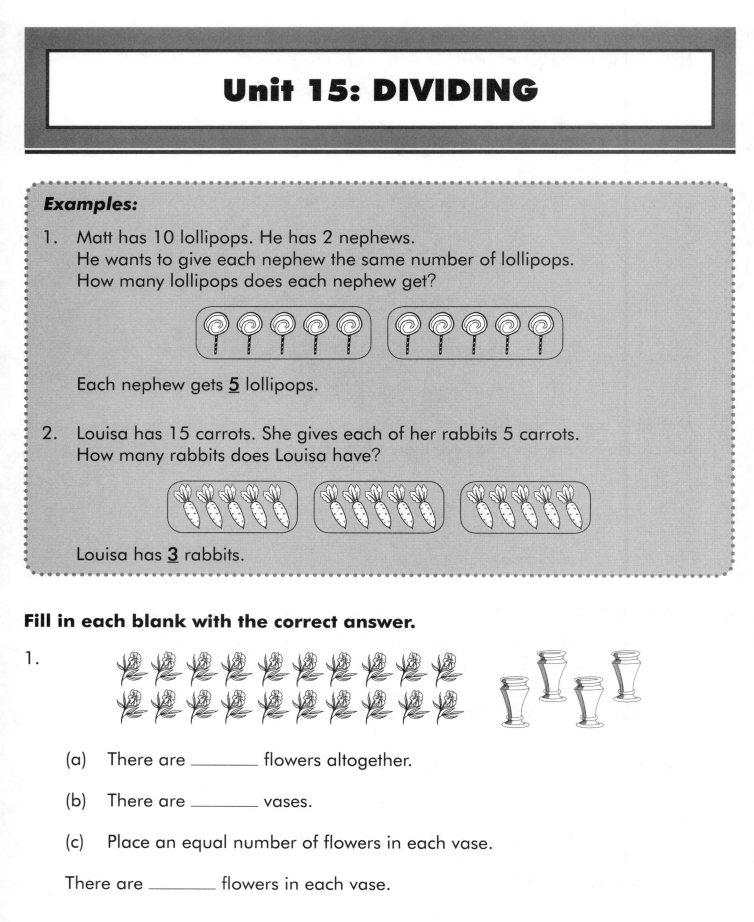

Examples:

1. Matt has 10 lollipops. He has 2 nephews.
    He wants to give each nephew the same number of lollipops.
    How many lollipops does each nephew get?

    Each nephew gets **5** lollipops.

2. Louisa has 15 carrots. She gives each of her rabbits 5 carrots.
    How many rabbits does Louisa have?

    Louisa has **3** rabbits.

Fill in each blank with the correct answer.

1.

(a) There are _____ flowers altogether.

(b) There are _____ vases.

(c) Place an equal number of flowers in each vase.

There are _____ flowers in each vase.

Singapore Math Practice Level 1B

2.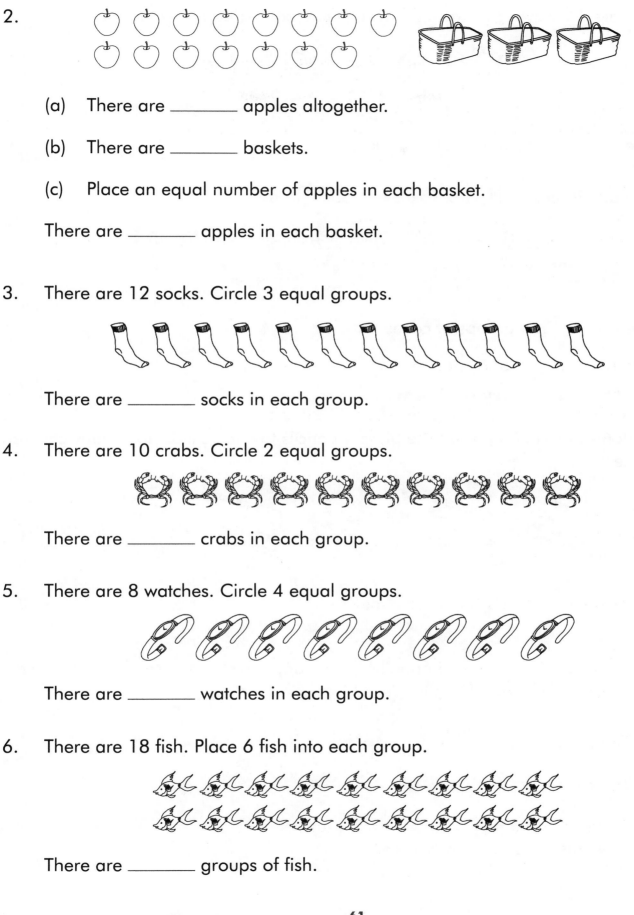

   (a)   There are _____ apples altogether.

   (b)   There are _____ baskets.

   (c)   Place an equal number of apples in each basket.

   There are _____ apples in each basket.

3. There are 12 socks. Circle 3 equal groups.

   There are _____ socks in each group.

4. There are 10 crabs. Circle 2 equal groups.

   There are _____ crabs in each group.

5. There are 8 watches. Circle 4 equal groups.

   There are _____ watches in each group.

6. There are 18 fish. Place 6 fish into each group.

   There are _____ groups of fish.

7. There are 16 ladybugs. Place 4 ladybugs into each group.

There are _____ groups of ladybugs.

8. There are 20 cakes. Place 2 cakes into each group.

There are _____ groups of cakes.

Solve the following story problems.

9. Mrs. James buys 20 pencils. She gives 4 pencils to each child. How many children are there?

There are _____ children.

10. 3 boys share 12 strawberries equally. How many strawberries does each boy get?

Each boy gets _____ strawberries.

Singapore Math Practice Level 1B

11. Ms. McKay bakes 18 cupcakes. She gives an equal number of cupcakes to 9 students. How many cupcakes does each student receive?

Each student receives _____ cupcakes.

12. Mr. Ramirez cuts a pizza into 10 slices. The pizza is shared equally among some people. If each person gets 2 slices of pizza, how many people share the pizza?

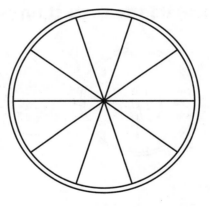

_____ people share the pizza.

Unit 16: TIME

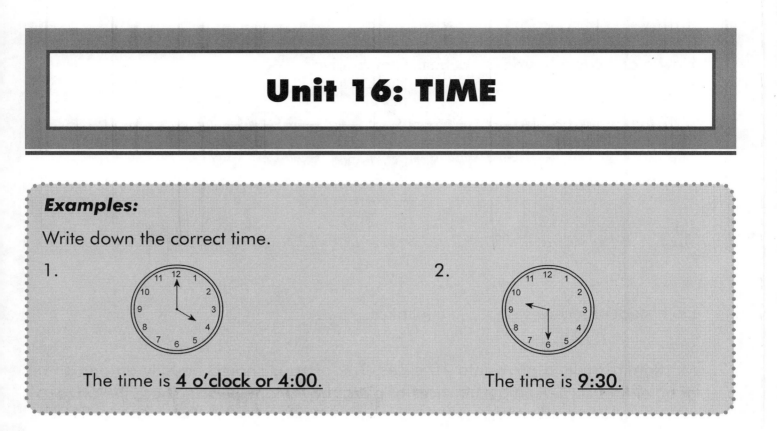

Examples:

Write down the correct time.

1.

The time is **4 o'clock or 4:00**.

2.

The time is **9:30**.

Read the time on each clock. Write the correct time on the lines.

1.

_____

2.

_____

3.

_____

4.

_____

5.

_____

6.

_____

Singapore Math Practice Level 1B

7. _____

8. _____

9. _____

Match each clock to the correct time.

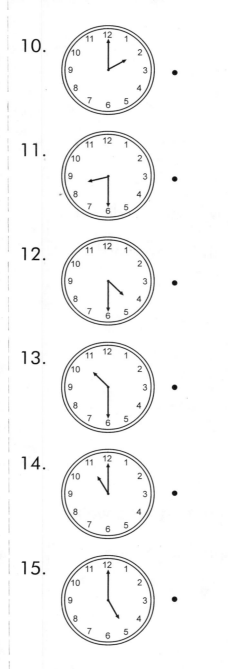

10.

11.

12.

13.

14.

15.

- 5 o'clock, 5:00

- 2 o'clock, 2:00

- 11 o'clock, 11:00

- 4:30

- 8:30

- 10:30

Singapore Math Practice Level 1B

Look at the clock in each picture. Fill in each blank with the correct answer.

16.

Anna-Maria has her breakfast at

_____ in the morning.

17.

John and his family have their dinner

at _____ in the evening.

18.

Samantha takes her dog for a walk

at _____ in the evening.

Singapore Math Practice Level 1B

19.

Colton has to feed his fish at

_____ every evening.

20.

Elizabeth goes to bed at

_____ every night.

21.

Brady walks to school at

_____ .

Singapore Math Practice Level 1B

REVIEW 3

Write the correct time on the lines below.

1.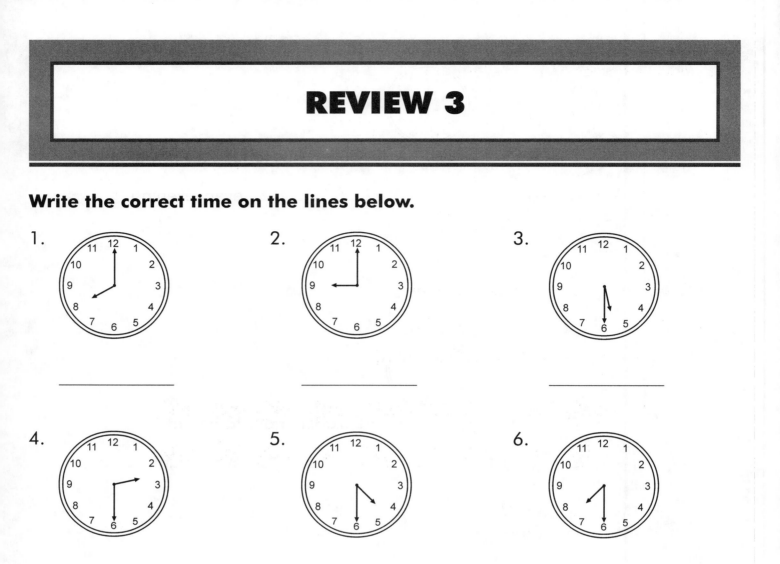

   _____

2.

   _____

3.

   _____

4.

   _____

5.

   _____

6.

   _____

Fill in each blank with the correct answer.

7.

   Molly has 18 bars of chocolate. She gives equal numbers of chocolate bars to her

   6 friends. Each friend receives _____ bars of chocolate.

Singapore Math Practice Level 1B

8. There are 20 apples.
   Place 4 apples on each plate.

There are _____ plates of apples.

9. There are 18 bows. Each girl has 3 bows.

There are _____ girls.

10. There are 16 balloons. Each child has 4 balloons.

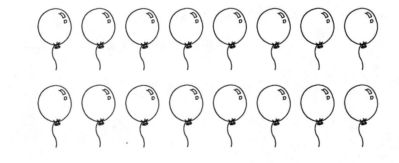

There are _____ children.

Singapore Math Practice Level 1B

Fill in the correct time on the lines below.

11.

Yoko goes to the library

at _____.

12.

Chris goes to school

at _____.

13.

Mom wakes up

at _____.

14.

Eli eats his lunch

at _____.

15.

Kaitlyn sleeps at _____.

16.

Anthony goes to the park

at _____.

Singapore Math Practice Level 1B

Solve the following story problems.

17. Winnie has 20 stickers. She gives an equal number of stickers to 5 of her friends. How many stickers does each friend receive?

Each friend receives _____ stickers.

18. Raj and his 2 friends caught 18 fish. They shared the fish equally. How many fish did each boy get?

Each boy got _____ fish.

19. Billy has 16 toy soldiers. He wants to put an equal number of toy soldiers into 2 boxes. How many toy soldiers are there in each box?

There are _____ toy soldiers in each box.

20. Alexandra buys 20 flowers. She places 4 flowers into each vase. How many vases does she need?

She needs _____ vases.

Singapore Math Practice Level 1B

Unit 17: NUMBERS 1–100

Examples:

1.

92	78	60	43

(a) The largest number is **92**.

(b) The smallest number is **43**.

(c) **60** is greater than 43 but smaller than 78.

(d) **78** is smaller than 92 but greater than 60.

2. Add 81 and 15.

$$81 + 15 = \underline{\textbf{96}}$$

	Tens	Ones
	8	1
+	1	5
	9	6

3. What is 79 − 34?

$$79 - 34 = \underline{\textbf{45}}$$

	Tens	Ones
	7	9
−	3	4
	4	5

4. What is 81 − 49?

$$81 - 49 = \underline{\textbf{32}}$$

	Tens	Ones
	^{7}8	^{11}1
−	4	9
	3	2

Singapore Math Practice Level 1B

Fill in each blank with the correct answer.

1. Write the following numbers in words.

    (a) 75 _____

    (b) 96 _____

    (c) 63 _____

    (d) 55 _____

    (e) 81 _____

    (f) 100 _____

2. Write the numbers on the lines below.

    (a) fifty   _____   (d) eighty-five _____

    (b) ninety-two   _____   (e) seventy-six _____

    (c) sixty-four   _____   (f) ninety-nine _____

Count the items. Write the correct answer in each blank.

3.

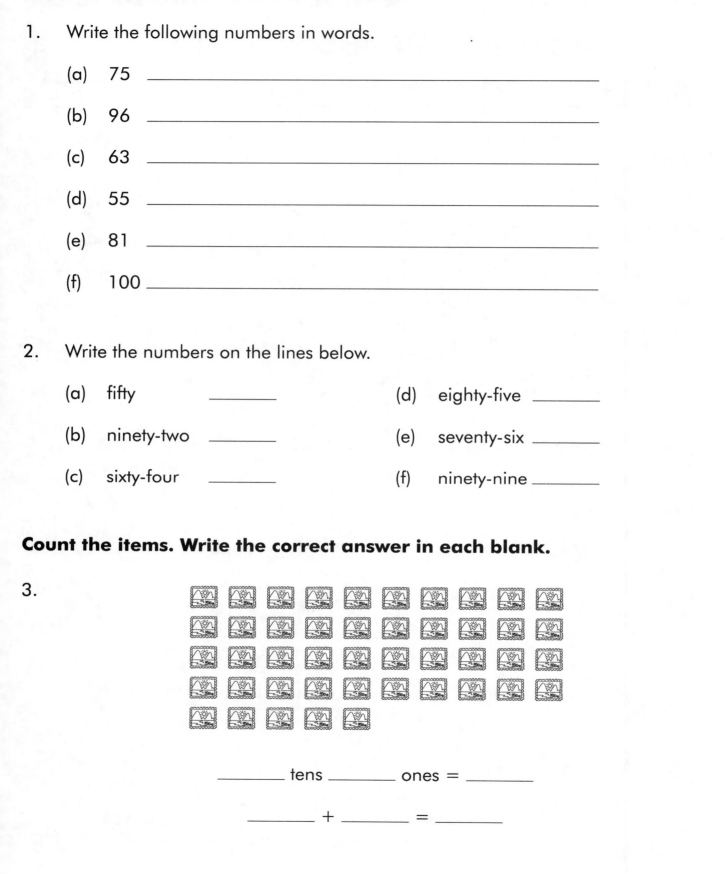

_____ tens _____ ones = _____

_____ + _____ = _____

Singapore Math Practice Level 1B

4.

_____ tens _____ ones = _____

_____ + _____ = _____

5.

_____ tens _____ ones = _____

_____ + _____ = _____

6.

_____ tens _____ ones = _____

_____ + _____ = _____

Singapore Math Practice Level 1B

7.

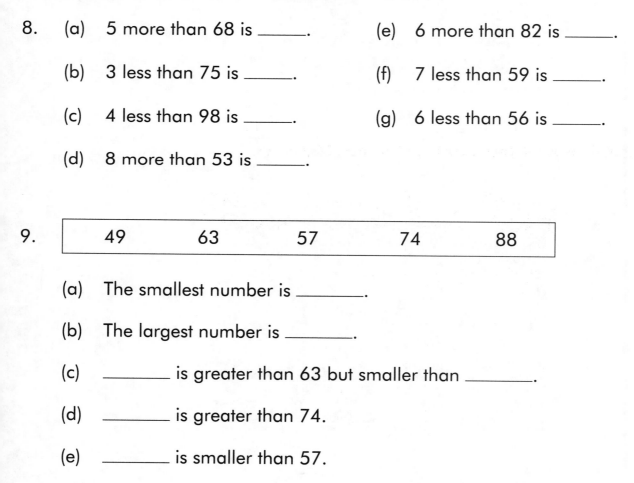

_____ tens _____ ones = _____

_____ + _____ = _____

Fill in each blank with the correct answer.

8. (a) 5 more than 68 is _____. (e) 6 more than 82 is _____.

(b) 3 less than 75 is _____. (f) 7 less than 59 is _____.

(c) 4 less than 98 is _____. (g) 6 less than 56 is _____.

(d) 8 more than 53 is _____.

9.

| 49 | 63 | 57 | 74 | 88 |

(a) The smallest number is _____.

(b) The largest number is _____.

(c) _____ is greater than 63 but smaller than _____.

(d) _____ is greater than 74.

(e) _____ is smaller than 57.

Singapore Math Practice Level 1B

10.

96	76	82	64	79

(a) The largest number is _____.

(b) The smallest number is _____.

(c) 3 more than 79 is _____.

(d) _____ is greater than 76 but smaller than 82.

(e) _____ is greater than 82.

11. Complete the number patterns.

(a) 80, 84, _____, _____, 96, _____

(b) 66, _____, 72, 75, _____, _____

(c) _____, _____, 84, 89, 94

Solve the addition problems below by making tens.

12. (a)

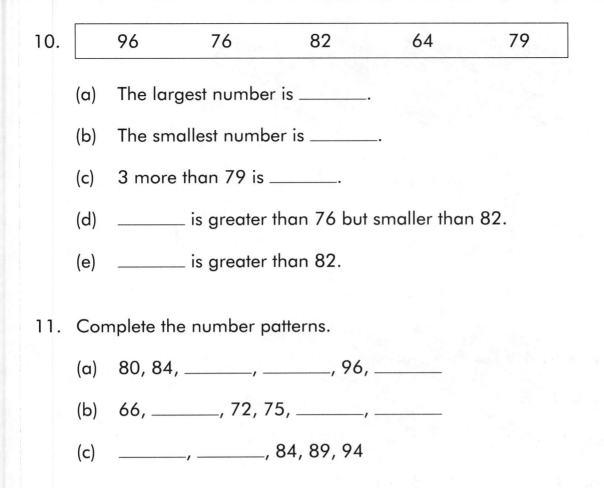

$42 + 4 =$ _____

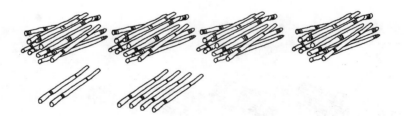

(b)

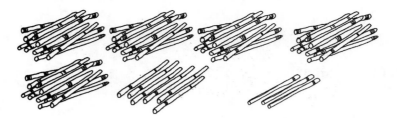

$$56 + 3 = \underline{\hphantom{XXXX}}$$

(c)

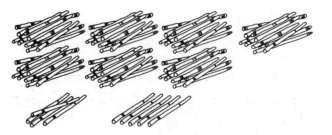

$$74 + 5 = \underline{\hphantom{XXXX}}$$

(d)

$$35 + 30 = \underline{\hphantom{XXXX}}$$

Singapore Math Practice Level 1B

(e)

$68 + 20 =$ _____

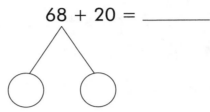

(f)

$84 + 10 =$ _____

Solve these addition problems by first grouping tens and ones.

13. (a) $37 + 8 =$ _____ tens _____ ones + _____ ones

    = _____ tens _____ ones

    Regroup the ones.

    = _____ tens _____ ones

    = _____

Singapore Math Practice Level 1B

(b) 45 + 5 = _____ tens _____ ones + _____ ones

   = _____ tens _____ ones

   Regroup the ones.

   = _____ tens _____ ones

   = _____

(c) 63 + 9 = _____ tens _____ ones + _____ ones

   = _____ tens _____ ones

   Regroup the ones.

   = _____ tens _____ ones

   = _____

(d) 74 + 13 = _____ tens _____ ones + _____ ones

   = _____ tens _____ ones

   Regroup the ones.

   = _____ tens _____ ones

   = _____

(e) 86 + 14 = _____ tens _____ ones + _____ ones

   = _____ tens _____ ones

   Regroup the ones.

   = _____ tens _____ ones

   = _____

(f) 58 + 22 = _____ tens _____ ones + _____ ones

   = _____ tens _____ ones

   Regroup the ones.

   = _____ tens _____ ones

   = _____

Singapore Math Practice Level 1B

14. (a)
$$53 + 14$$

(e)
$$28 + 64$$

(b)
$$70 + 28$$

(f)
$$35 + 47$$

(c)
$$91 + 6$$

(g)
$$68 + 18$$

(d)
$$44 + 34$$

(h)
$$86 + 9$$

15. Match each cyclist to the correct bicycle.

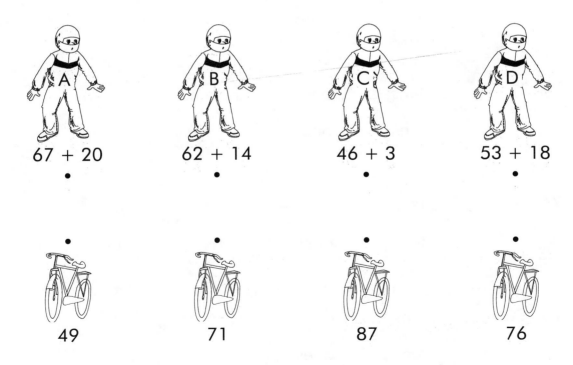

A
67 + 20

B
62 + 14

C
46 + 3

D
53 + 18

49   71   87   76

Solve these subtraction problems by first grouping tens and ones.

16. (a)   64 – 3 = _____

(b)   89 – 6 = _____

(c)   93 – 4 = _____

(d)   77 – 5 = _____

(e)   54 – 6 = _____

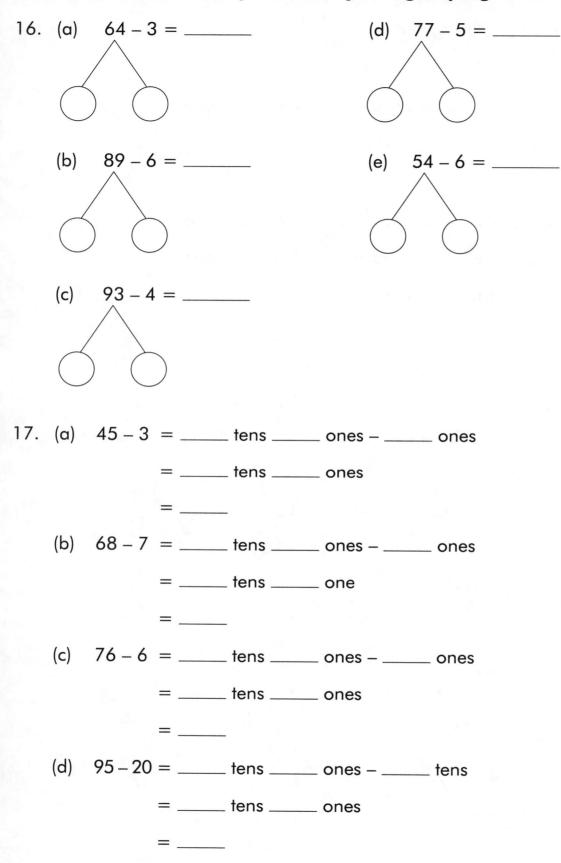

17. (a)   45 – 3 = _____ tens _____ ones – _____ ones

       = _____ tens _____ ones

       = _____

(b)   68 – 7 = _____ tens _____ ones – _____ ones

       = _____ tens _____ one

       = _____

(c)   76 – 6 = _____ tens _____ ones – _____ ones

       = _____ tens _____ ones

       = _____

(d)   95 – 20 = _____ tens _____ ones – _____ tens

       = _____ tens _____ ones

       = _____

Singapore Math Practice Level 1B

(e) $84 - 30 = $ _____ tens _____ ones – _____ tens

$\qquad = $ _____ tens _____ ones

$\qquad = $ _____

(f) $93 - 12 = $ _____ tens _____ ones – _____ ten _____ ones

$\qquad = $ _____ tens _____ one

$\qquad = $ _____

(g) $56 - 17 = $ _____ tens _____ ones – _____ ten _____ ones

$\qquad = $ _____ tens _____ ones – _____ ten _____ ones

$\qquad = $ _____ tens _____ ones

$\qquad = $ _____

18. (a)
```
   9 7
 - 3 6
 _____
```

(b)
```
   7 8
 - 1 2
 _____
```

(c)
```
   4 6
 - 2 5
 _____
```

(d)
```
   8 9
 - 5 4
 _____
```

(e)
```
   6 0
 - 3 7
 _____
```

(f)
```
   5 5
 - 2 8
 _____
```

(g)
```
   9 2
 - 4 6
 _____
```

(h)
```
   7 1
 - 1 7
 _____
```

Singapore Math Practice Level 1B

19. Match each helmet to the correct child.

Solve the story problems below.

20. Jake has 80 toy soldiers. Demetrius has 10 fewer toy soldiers. How many toy soldiers does Demetrius have?

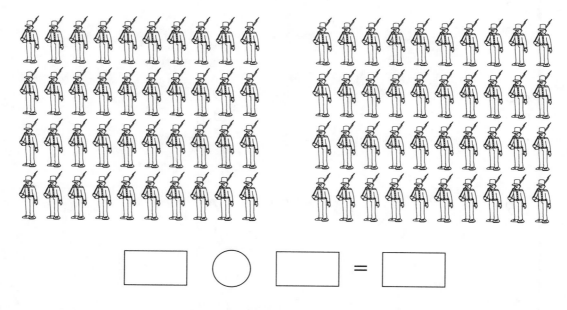

Demetrius has _____ toy soldiers.

Singapore Math Practice Level 1B

21. Chloe collects 65 stamps. Rachel collects 8 fewer stamps. How many stamps does Rachel collect?

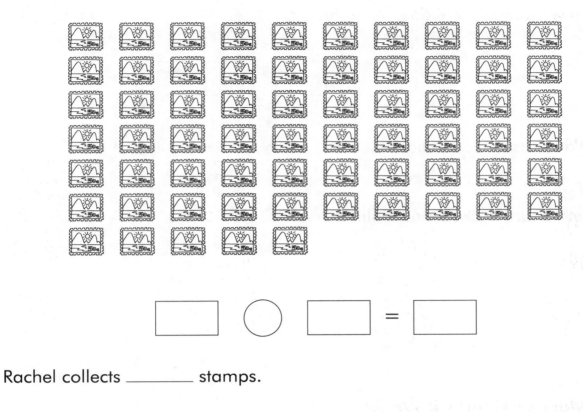

Rachel collects _____ stamps.

22. Logan has 72 bottle caps. He has 18 fewer bottle caps than Justin. How many bottle caps does Justin have?

Justin has _____ bottle caps.

23. Sasha has 18 stickers. Akira has 10 fewer stickers than Sasha. Julia has 3 stickers more than Akira.

(a) How many stickers does Akira have?

$$\boxed{} \;\bigcirc\; \boxed{} \;=\; \boxed{}$$

Akira has _____ stickers.

(b) How many stickers does Julia have?

$$\boxed{} \;\bigcirc\; \boxed{} \;=\; \boxed{}$$

Julia has _____ stickers.

(c) Who has the fewest stickers?

_____ has the fewest stickers.

Singapore Math Practice Level 1B

Unit 18: MONEY (PART 1)

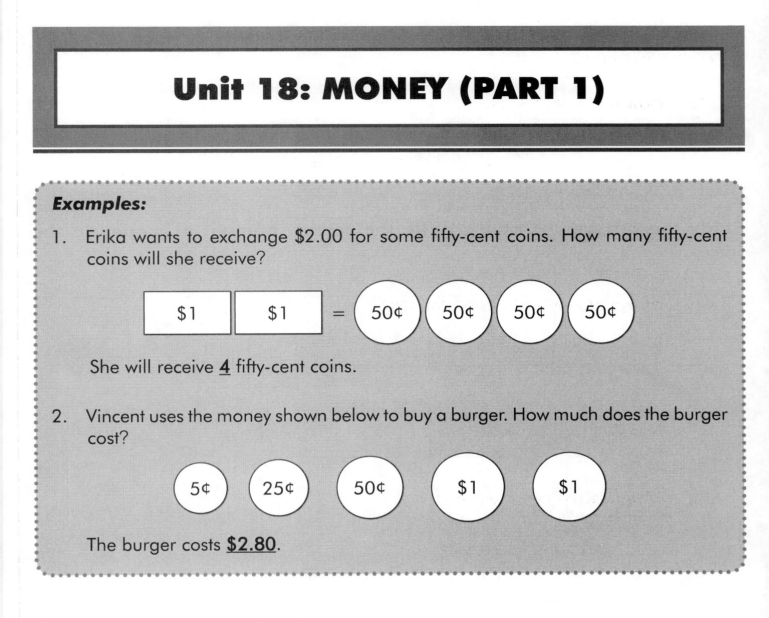

Examples:

1. Erika wants to exchange $2.00 for some fifty-cent coins. How many fifty-cent coins will she receive?

   | $1 | $1 | = (50¢) (50¢) (50¢) (50¢)

   She will receive **4** fifty-cent coins.

2. Vincent uses the money shown below to buy a burger. How much does the burger cost?

   (5¢) (25¢) (50¢) ($1) ($1)

   The burger costs **$2.80**.

Fill in each blank with the correct answer.

1. 50¢ = _____ ten-cent coins

2. $1 = _____ fifty-cent coins

3. $5 = _____ one-dollar coins

4. $10 = _____ five-dollar bills

5. 10¢ = _____ five-cent coins

6. $50 = _____ ten-dollar bills

Singapore Math Practice Level 1B

7. $2 = _____ fifty-cent coins

8. $1 = _____ twenty-five-cent coins

9. $50 = _____ five-dollar bills

10. $1 = _____ five-cent coins

Study the pictures carefully. Write the correct amount of money in the boxes.

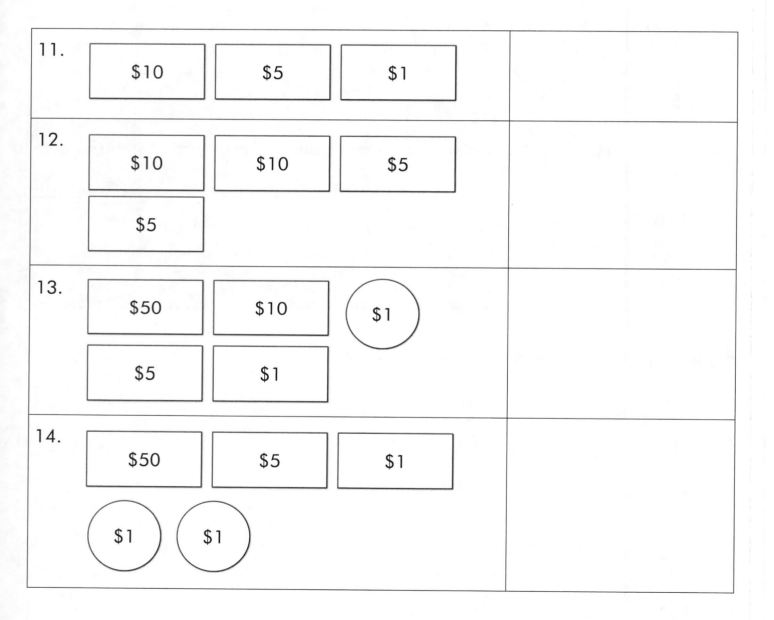

Singapore Math Practice Level 1B

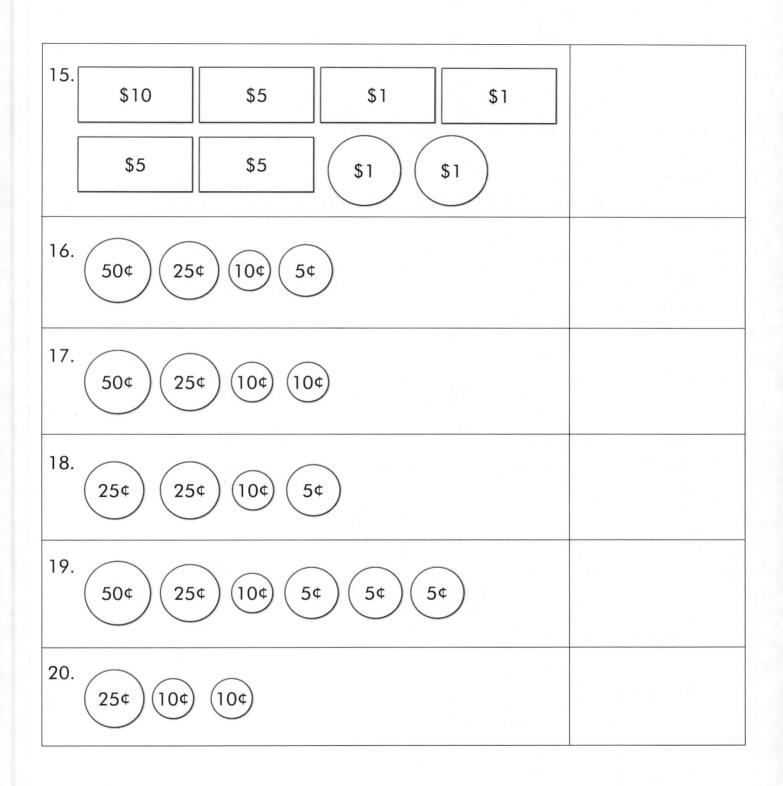

15.

| $10 | $5 | $1 | $1 |

| $5 | $5 | $1 | $1 |

16.

50¢ 25¢ 10¢ 5¢

17.

50¢ 25¢ 10¢ 10¢

18.

25¢ 25¢ 10¢ 5¢

19.

50¢ 25¢ 10¢ 5¢ 5¢ 5¢

20.

25¢ 10¢ 10¢

Look at each picture, and color the amount of money you would need to purchase the item shown.

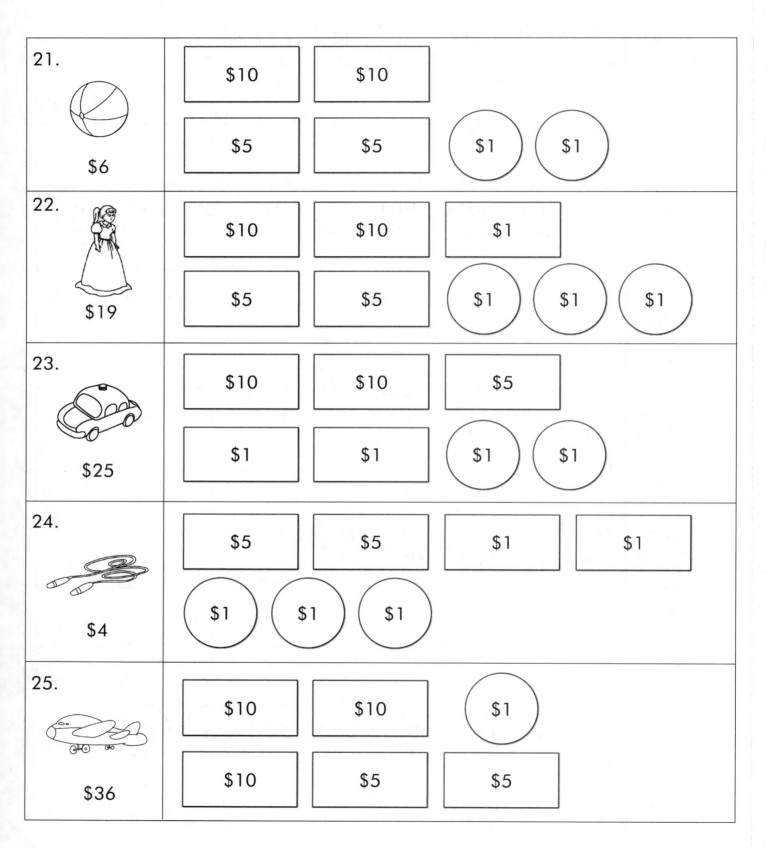

21.
$6

| $10 | $10 |
| $5 | $5 | $1 $1 |

22.
$19

| $10 | $10 | $1 |
| $5 | $5 | $1 $1 $1 |

23.
$25

| $10 | $10 | $5 |
| $1 | $1 | $1 $1 |

24.
$4

| $5 | $5 | $1 | $1 |
| $1 $1 $1 |

25.
$36

| $10 | $10 | $1 |
| $10 | $5 | $5 |

Singapore Math Practice Level 1B

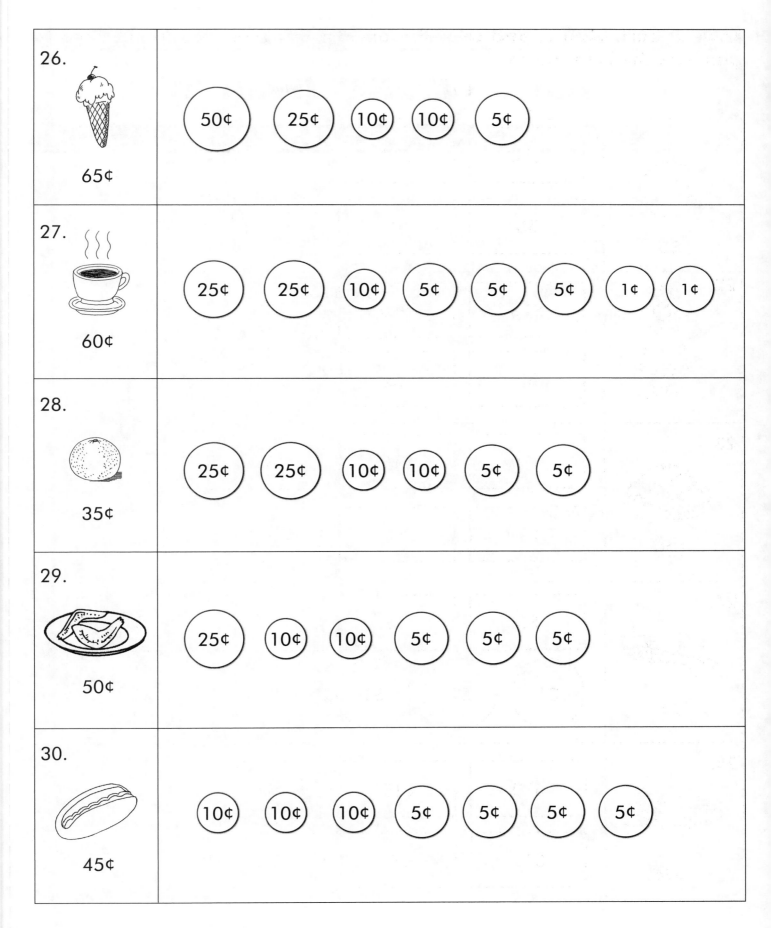

26. 65¢

50¢ 25¢ 10¢ 10¢ 5¢

27. 60¢

25¢ 25¢ 10¢ 5¢ 5¢ 5¢ 1¢ 1¢

28. 35¢

25¢ 25¢ 10¢ 10¢ 5¢ 5¢

29. 50¢

25¢ 10¢ 10¢ 5¢ 5¢ 5¢

30. 45¢

10¢ 10¢ 10¢ 5¢ 5¢ 5¢ 5¢

Singapore Math Practice Level 1B

Unit 19: MONEY (PART 2)

1. Angelo buys 2 pieces of fruit in the school cafeteria.
   A piece of watermelon costs 50¢.
   An orange costs 30¢ more than the watermelon.
   How much is the orange?

$$50¢ + 30¢ = 80¢$$

   The orange is **80¢**.

2. Noelle buys a skirt that costs $38.
   She gives the cashier $50.
   How much change will she receive?

$$\$50 - \$38 = \$12$$

   She will receive **$12**.

Singapore Math Practice Level 1B

Unit 10: Mass

1. **lighter than**
    When the apple on the balance moves upward, this shows it is lighter.
2. **heavier than**
    When the keyboard on the balance moves downward, this shows it is heavier.
3. **as heavy as**
    When the balance is equal, this shows that the apple and mango have the same mass.
4. **3**
5. **5**
6. **6**
7. **10**
8. **4**
9. **7**
10. **3**
11. **5**
12. **dictionary**
    The mass of the book is 5 units, and the mass of the dictionary is 7 units.
13. **box of pencils**
    The mass of the box of pencils is 3 units, and the mass of the file is 4 units.
14. **dictionary**
15. **box of pencils**
16. **box of pencils, notebook, book, dictionary**
17. **7**
18. **5**
19. **4**
20. **2**
21. **kite**
    The mass of the doll is 4 units, and the mass of the kite is 2 units.
22. **teddy bear**
    The mass of the teddy bear is 7 units, and the mass of the toy car is 5 units.
23. **kite**
24. **teddy bear**
25. **doll**
26. **11**
27. **9**
28. **10**
29. **B**
    The mass of Basket C is 10 units, and the mass of Basket B is 9 units.
30. **A**
    The mass of Basket A is 11 units, and the mass of Basket C is 10 units.
31. **A**
32. **B**
33. **A, C, B**

34. **D**
35. **B**
36. **11**
37. **12**
38. **B**
    The mass of Bag C is 8 units, and the mass of Bag B is 7 units.
39. **A**
    The mass of Bag D is 12 units, the mass of Bag A is 11 units, and the mass of Bag C is 8 units.
40. **D, A, C, B**

Unit 11: Picture Graphs

1. | Monkeys | ● ● ● ● ● ● |
    |---------|------------|
    | Lions | ● ● ● |
    | Tigers | ● ● |
    | Giraffes | ● ● ● ● |
    | Parrots | ● ● |

2. | Hopscotch | Soccer | Jumping Rope | Marbles |
    |-----------|--------|--------------|---------|
    | ★★★ | ★★★★★★★★★ | ★★★ | ★★★★★ |

3. | Soccer | ▲ ▲ ▲ ▲ ▲ ▲ ▲ |
    |--------|----------------|
    | Kite-Flying | ▲ ▲ ▲ ▲ |
    | Feeding Ducks | ▲ ▲ |
    | Walking | ▲ ▲ ▲ ▲ ▲ |

4. **4**
5. **5**
6. **turkey burgers**
7. **chicken fingers**
8. $4 - 2 = $ **2**
9. $5 - 3 = $ **2**
10. **6**
11. **10**
12. **football**
13. **karate**
14. **swimming, baseball**
15. $7 - 4 = $ **3**
16. $10 - 4 = $ **6**

17. 7 + 6 + 10 = 23
    23 + 6 + 4 = **33**
18. **4**
19. **2**
20. **ants**
21. **ladybugs**
22. 7 − 4 = **3**
23. 5 − 2 = **3**
24. 4 + 5 + 7 = 16
    16 + 2 = **18**

Review 1

1. **8**
2. **5**
3. **thermos**
4. **coffee pot**
5. 8 − 5 = **3**
6. 10 − 7 = **3**
7. **5**
8. **2**
9. **6**
10. **9**
11. **D**
12. **B**
13.

	★		★
★	★		★
★	★	★	★
★	★	★	★
★	★	★	★
Kite-Flying	Riding Bikes	Feeding Birds	Walking
Each ★ stands for 1 student.			

14. **heavier than**
    When the book on the balance moves downward, this shows it is heavier.
15. **lighter than**
    When the glass on the balance moves upward, this shows it is lighter.
16. **as heavy as**
    When the balance is equal, this shows that the water bottle and telephone have the same mass.
17. **heavier than**
    When the picture frame on the balance moves downward, this shows it is heavier.
18. **8**
19. **12**
20. **3**

Unit 12: Numbers up to 40

1. **26**

2. **13**

3. **30**

4. **31**

5. **21**

6. (a) **twenty**
   (b) **fifteen**
   (c) **thirty-nine**
   (d) **twenty-seven**
   (e) **eleven**
   (f) **forty**
   (g) **thirty-five**
   (h) **twenty-one**
7. (a) **14**
   (b) **24**
   (c) **30**
   (d) **19**
   (e) **26**
   (f) **18**
   (g) **32**
   (h) **13**
8. (a) 30 + 6 = **36**
   (b) 20 + 1 = **21**
   (c) 10 + 7 = **17**
   (d) 20 + 8 = **28**
   (e) 30 + 3 = **33**
   (f) 10 + 4 = **14**
   (g) 20 + 6 = **26**
   (h) 30 + 9 = **39**
9. **3, 5, 35**
10. **2, 1, 21**
11. **3, 9, 39**
12. **4, 0, 40**
13. **1, 6, 16**
14. **2, 3, 23**
15. 2 + 16 = **18**
16. 35 − 5 = **30**
17. 3 + 24 = **27**
18. 1 + 39 = **40**
19. 28 − 9 = **19**
20. (a) **35**
    (b) **17**
    (c) **35**
    (d) **17**
    (e) **17, 22, 35**

21. (a) **16**
 (b) **40**
 (c) 2 + 29 = **31**
 (d) 29 − 2 = **27**
 (e) **27, 31**
22. (a) **40**
 (b) **19**
 (c) 2 + 19 = **21**
 (d) 40 − 5 = **35**
 (e) **21**
23. (a) **14**
 (b) **31**
 (c) 3 + 28 = **31**
 (d) 17 − 3 = **14**
 (e) **25**

24. 2 less than 21   38
25. 1 more than 37   24
26. 3 more than 20   19
27. 2 more than 23   15
28. 3 less than 18   23
29. 1 less than 25   25

30. **11, 17**
 23 − 20 = 3
 14 − 3 = 11
 14 + 3 = 17
31. **24, 29**
 14 − 9 = 5
 19 + 5 = 24
 24 + 5 = 29
32. **30, 40**
 25 + 5 = 30
 35 + 5 = 40
33. **30, 36**
 34 − 32 = 2
 28 + 2 = 30
 34 + 2 = 36
34. **36, 42**
 24 − 18 = 6
 30 + 6 = 36
 36 + 6 = 42

35. **29**
```
    2 0
 +    9
    2 9
```
36. **13**
```
    1 0
 +    3
    1 3
```
37. **24**
```
    2 0
 +    4
    2 4
```
38. **37**
```
    3 0
 +    7
    3 7
```
39. **34**
```
    3 0
 +    4
    3 4
```

40. (a) **3, 4, 2**
 3, 6
 36
 (b) **1, 6, 4**
 1, 10
 20
 (c) **2, 2, 7**
 2, 9
 29
 (d) **2, 4, 8**
 2, 12
 32
 (e) **2, 7, 7**
 2, 14
 34

41. (a)
Tens	Ones
1	3
+ 1	3
2	**6**

 (b)
Tens	Ones
2	4
+ 1	5
3	**9**

 (c)
Tens	Ones
3	5
+	2
3	**7**

 (d)
Tens	Ones
1	1
+ 2	6
3	**7**

 (e)
Tens	Ones
3	0
+	6
3	**6**

42. (a)
Tens	Ones
¹2	9
+	7
3	**6**

 (b)
Tens	Ones
¹1	5
+ 1	8
3	**3**

 (c)
Tens	Ones
¹2	8
+ 1	2
4	**0**

 (d)
Tens	Ones
¹1	9
+ 1	6
3	**5**

 (e)
Tens	Ones
¹2	5
+	6
3	**1**

Singapore Math Practice Level 1B

43.

Houses: 36, 24, 17, 33, 29

10 + 7   33 + 3   21 + 8   17 + 7   29 + 4

A   B   C   D   E

$$
\begin{array}{r} 1\,0 \\ +\ 7 \\ \hline 1\,7 \end{array}
\qquad
\begin{array}{r} 3\,3 \\ +\ 3 \\ \hline 3\,6 \end{array}
\qquad
\begin{array}{r} 2\,1 \\ +\ 8 \\ \hline 2\,9 \end{array}
\qquad
\begin{array}{r} {}^1 1\,7 \\ +\ 7 \\ \hline 2\,4 \end{array}
\qquad
\begin{array}{r} {}^1 2\,9 \\ +\ 4 \\ \hline 3\,3 \end{array}
$$

44.

(a) $27 - 3 = \mathbf{24}$

   (20) (7)

$7 - 3 = 4$
$20 + 4 = 24$

(b) $36 - 2 = \mathbf{34}$

   (30) (6)

$6 - 2 = 4$
$30 + 4 = 34$

(c) $19 - 3 = \mathbf{16}$

   (10) (9)

$9 - 3 = 6$
$10 + 6 = 16$

(d) $25 - 4 = \mathbf{21}$

   (20) (5)

$5 - 4 = 1$
$20 + 1 = 21$

(e) $38 - 9 = \mathbf{29}$

   (28) (10)

$10 - 9 = 1$
$28 + 1 = 29$

(f) $30 - 3 = \mathbf{27}$

   (20) (10)

$10 - 3 = 7$
$20 + 7 = 27$

45.

(a) **2, 6, 2**
2, 4
24

(b) **3, 7, 3**
3, 4
34

(c) **1, 6, 1**
1, 5
15

(d) **2, 4, 4**
2, 0
20

(e) **3, 3, 4**
2, 13, 4
2, 9
29

46.

(a)
Tens	Ones
2	8
−	7
2	**1**

(b)
Tens	Ones
3	5
− 1	2
2	**3**

(c)
Tens	Ones
1	9
−	6
1	**3**

(d)
Tens	Ones
2	5
− 1	1
1	**4**

(e)
Tens	Ones
3	7
− 1	3
2	**4**

47.

(a)
Tens	Ones
²2̸	¹²2̸
− 1	8
1	**4**

(b)
Tens	Ones
³2̸	¹⁰0̸
− 1	5
2	**5**

(c)
Tens	Ones
¹2̸	¹⁶6̸
− 1	7
	9

(d)
Tens	Ones
¹2̸	¹³3̸
− 1	4
	9

(e)
Tens	Ones
²2̸	¹⁰0̸
−	9
2	**1**

48.

Houses: 22, 27, 32, 10, 18

36 − 4   28 − 6   17 − 7   34 − 7   22 − 4

A   B   C   D   E

$$
\begin{array}{r} 3\,6 \\ -\ 4 \\ \hline 3\,2 \end{array}
\qquad
\begin{array}{r} 2\,8 \\ -\ 6 \\ \hline 2\,2 \end{array}
\qquad
\begin{array}{r} 1\,7 \\ -\ 7 \\ \hline 1\,0 \end{array}
\qquad
\begin{array}{r} {}^2 3̸\,{}^{14}4̸ \\ -\ 7 \\ \hline 2\,7 \end{array}
\qquad
\begin{array}{r} {}^1 2̸\,{}^{12}2̸ \\ -\ 4 \\ \hline 1\,8 \end{array}
$$

49. $3 + 5 + 7 = \mathbf{15}$

  (2) (3)
    (10)

$7 + 3 = 10$
$3 + 2 = 5$
$10 + 5 = 15$

Singapore Math Practice Level 1B

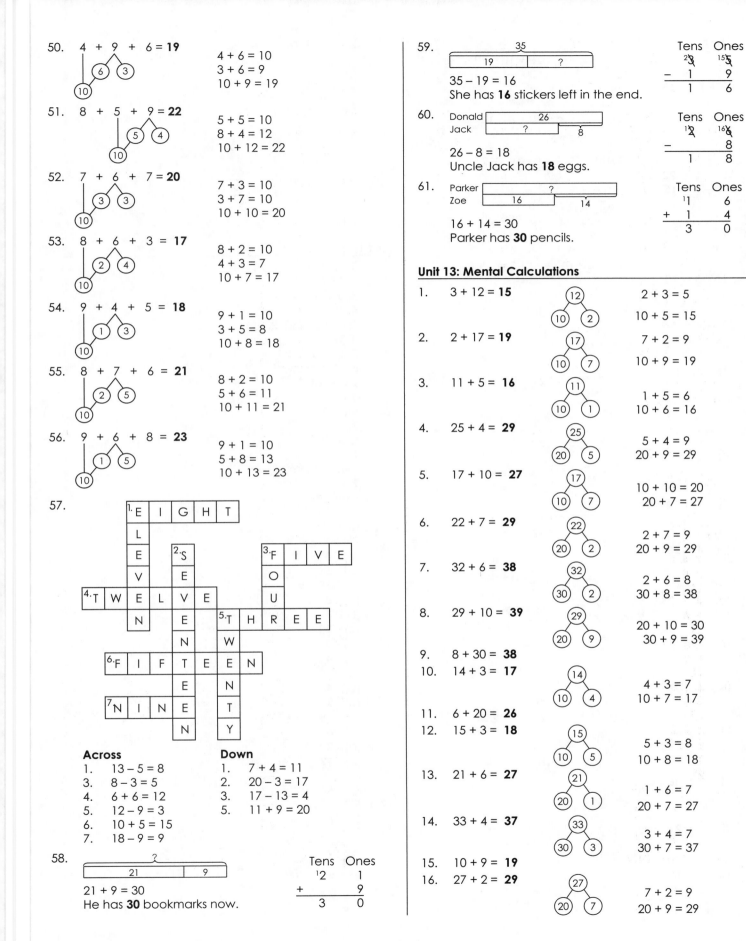

50. $4 + 9 + 6 = \textbf{19}$

6 3
10

$4 + 6 = 10$
$3 + 6 = 9$
$10 + 9 = 19$

51. $8 + 5 + 9 = \textbf{22}$

5 4
10

$5 + 5 = 10$
$8 + 4 = 12$
$10 + 12 = 22$

52. $7 + 6 + 7 = \textbf{20}$

3 3
10

$7 + 3 = 10$
$3 + 7 = 10$
$10 + 10 = 20$

53. $8 + 6 + 3 = \textbf{17}$

2 4
10

$8 + 2 = 10$
$4 + 3 = 7$
$10 + 7 = 17$

54. $9 + 4 + 5 = \textbf{18}$

1 3
10

$9 + 1 = 10$
$3 + 5 = 8$
$10 + 8 = 18$

55. $8 + 7 + 6 = \textbf{21}$

2 5
10

$8 + 2 = 10$
$5 + 6 = 11$
$10 + 11 = 21$

56. $9 + 6 + 8 = \textbf{23}$

1 5
10

$9 + 1 = 10$
$5 + 8 = 13$
$10 + 13 = 23$

57.

Crossword:
1. E I G H T
   L
   E 2.S 3.F I V E
   V E   O
4.T W E L V E U
   N E 5.T H R E E
      N W
6.F I F T E E N
      E N
7.N I N E T
      N Y

Across
1. $13 - 5 = 8$
3. $8 - 3 = 5$
4. $6 + 6 = 12$
5. $12 - 9 = 3$
6. $10 + 5 = 15$
7. $18 - 9 = 9$

Down
1. $7 + 4 = 11$
2. $20 - 3 = 17$
3. $17 - 13 = 4$
5. $11 + 9 = 20$

58.

| 21 | 9 |

$21 + 9 = 30$
He has **30** bookmarks now.

Tens Ones
^{12} 1
$+$ 9
3 0

59.

| 35 |
| 19 | ? |

$35 - 19 = 16$
She has **16** stickers left in the end.

Tens Ones
$^2\cancel{3}$ $^{15}\cancel{5}$
$-$ 1 9
1 6

60. Donald | 26 |
    Jack | ? | 8

$26 - 8 = 18$
Uncle Jack has **18** eggs.

Tens Ones
$^1\cancel{2}$ $^{16}\cancel{6}$
$-$ 8
1 8

61. Parker | ? |
    Zoe | 16 | 14

$16 + 14 = 30$
Parker has **30** pencils.

Tens Ones
^{11} 6
$+$ 1 4
3 0

Unit 13: Mental Calculations

1. $3 + 12 = \textbf{15}$

12
10 2

$2 + 3 = 5$
$10 + 5 = 15$

2. $2 + 17 = \textbf{19}$

17
10 7

$7 + 2 = 9$
$10 + 9 = 19$

3. $11 + 5 = \textbf{16}$

11
10 1

$1 + 5 = 6$
$10 + 6 = 16$

4. $25 + 4 = \textbf{29}$

25
20 5

$5 + 4 = 9$
$20 + 9 = 29$

5. $17 + 10 = \textbf{27}$

17
10 7

$10 + 10 = 20$
$20 + 7 = 27$

6. $22 + 7 = \textbf{29}$

22
20 2

$2 + 7 = 9$
$20 + 9 = 29$

7. $32 + 6 = \textbf{38}$

32
30 2

$2 + 6 = 8$
$30 + 8 = 38$

8. $29 + 10 = \textbf{39}$

29
20 9

$20 + 10 = 30$
$30 + 9 = 39$

9. $8 + 30 = \textbf{38}$

10. $14 + 3 = \textbf{17}$

14
10 4

$4 + 3 = 7$
$10 + 7 = 17$

11. $6 + 20 = \textbf{26}$

12. $15 + 3 = \textbf{18}$

15
10 5

$5 + 3 = 8$
$10 + 8 = 18$

13. $21 + 6 = \textbf{27}$

21
20 1

$1 + 6 = 7$
$20 + 7 = 27$

14. $33 + 4 = \textbf{37}$

33
30 3

$3 + 4 = 7$
$30 + 7 = 37$

15. $10 + 9 = \textbf{19}$

16. $27 + 2 = \textbf{29}$

27
20 7

$7 + 2 = 9$
$20 + 9 = 29$

17. 16 + 10 = **26**

(16) → (10) (6)

10 + 10 = 20
20 + 6 = 26

18. 7 + 11 = **18**

(11) → (10) (1)

1 + 7 = 8
10 + 8 = 18

19. 13 + 6 = **19**

(13) → (10) (3)

3 + 6 = 9
10 + 9 = 19

20. 20 + 2 = **22**

21. 18 − 3 = **15**

(18) → (10) (8)

8 − 3 = 5
10 + 5 = 15

22. 28 − 6 = **22**

(28) → (20) (8)

8 − 6 = 2
20 + 2 = 22

23. 15 − 5 = **10**

(15) → (10) (5)

5 − 5 = 0
10 + 0 = 10

24. 36 − 4 = **32**

(36) → (30) (6)

6 − 4 = 2
30 + 2 = 32

25. 14 − 10 = **4**

(14) → (4) (10)

10 − 10 = 0
0 + 4 = 4

26. 33 − 2 = **31**

(33) → (30) (3)

3 − 2 = 1
30 + 1 = 31

27. 16 − 3 = **13**

(16) → (10) (6)

6 − 3 = 3
10 + 3 = 13

28. 19 − 5 = **14**

(19) → (10) (9)

9 − 5 = 4
10 + 4 = 14

29. 24 − 4 = **20**

(24) → (20) (4)

4 − 4 = 0
20 + 0 = 20

30. 33 − 30 = **3**

(33) → (30) (3)

30 − 30 = 0
0 + 3 = 3

31. 39 − 20 = **19**

(39) → (30) (9)

30 − 20 = 10
10 + 9 = 19

32. 29 − 4 = **25**

(29) → (20) (9)

9 − 4 = 5
20 + 5 = 25

33. 17 − 2 = **15**

(17) → (10) (7)

7 − 2 = 5
10 + 5 = 15

34. 39 − 3 = **36**

(39) → (30) (9)

9 − 3 = 6
30 + 6 = 36

35. 23 − 2 = **21**

(23) → (20) (3)

3 − 2 = 1
20 + 1 = 21

36. 14 − 3 = **11**

(14) → (10) (4)

4 − 3 = 1
10 + 1 = 11

37. 28 − 10 = **18**

(28) → (20) (8)

20 − 10 = 10
10 + 8 = 18

38. 35 − 4 = **31**

(35) → (30) (5)

5 − 4 = 1
30 + 1 = 31

39. 37 − 10 = **27**

(37) → (30) (7)

30 − 10 = 20
20 + 7 = 27

40. 25 − 3 = **22**

(25) → (20) (5)

5 − 3 = 2
20 + 2 = 22

Unit 14: Multiplying

1. **5, 5, 5, 15**
   3, 15
2. **3, 3, 3, 3, 12**
   4, 12
3. **2, 2, 2, 2, 2, 2, 2, 2, 16**
   8, 16
4. **5, 5, 5, 5, 5, 25**
   5, 25
5. **sixes, 18**
   3, 18
6. **tens, 20**
   2, 20
7. **fours, 28**
   7, 28
8. **threes, 27**
   9, 27
9. **nines, 36**
   4, 36
10. **twos, 20**
    10, 20
11. (a) **3**
    (b) **6**
    (c) **18**
12. (a) **8**
    (b) **3**
    (c) **24**
13. (a) **5**
    (b) **4**
    (c) **20**
14. (a) **4**
    (b) **7**
    (c) **28**
15. (a) **6**
    (b) **2**
    (c) **12**
16. **3, 2**
    3, 2, 6
17. **5, 3**
    5, 3, 15
18. **7, 5**
    7, 5, 35
19. **8, 4**
    8, 4, 32
20. **6, 6**
    6, 6, 36

21. **4, 5, 20, 20**
22. **8, 3, 24, 24**
23. **3, 6, 18, 18**
24. **8, 4, 32, 32**
25. **5, 3, 15, 15**
26. **4, 5, 20, 20**
27. **9, 2, 18, 18**
28. **4, 7, 28, 28**
29. **3, 4, 12, 12**
30. **2, 8, 16, 16**

Review 2

1. (a) **12**
   (b) **28**
   (c) **35**
   (d) **11**
   (e) **16**
2. (a) **forty**
   (b) **twenty-nine**
   (c) **thirteen**
   (d) **thirty-eight**
   (e) **fifteen**
3. $20 - 5 =$ **15**
4. $1 + 39 =$ **40**
5. $27 - 3 =$ **24**
6. $4 + 15 =$ **19**
7. $17 - 2 =$ **15**
8. **5, 5, 5, 5, 5, 5, 30**
   fives, 30
9. **9, 9, 9, 27**
   nines, 27
10. (a) **16**
    (b) **31**
    (c) $25 + 3 =$ **28**
    (d) $22 - 3 =$ **19**
    (e) **25**
11. (a) **3, 6, 6**
       3, 0
       30
    (b) **2, 7, 9**
       1, 17, 9
       1, 8
       18
    (c) **1, 6, 7**
       0, 16, 7
       0, 9
       9
12. (a) **8, 24**
       $16 - 12 = 4$
       $12 - 4 = 8$
       $20 + 4 = 24$
    (b) **19, 22**
       $28 - 25 = 3$
       $25 - 3 = 22$
       $22 - 3 = 19$
13. (a)

Tens	Ones
1	2
+ 2	4
3	**6**

    (b)

Tens	Ones
1	5
+ 1	3
2	**8**

(c)

Tens	Ones
¹2	5
+	6
3	**1**

(d)

Tens	Ones
¹1	9
+ 1	7
3	**6**

14. (a)

Tens	Ones
1	9
−	8
1	**1**

(b)

Tens	Ones
2	7
− 1	4
1	**3**

(c)

Tens	Ones
³⁄4	¹⁰0
− 1	5
2	**5**

(d)

Tens	Ones
²3	¹⁵5
− 1	9
1	**6**

15. $31 + 7 =$ **38**
   $1 + 7 = 8$
   $30 + 8 = 38$
16. $28 - 10 =$ **18**
   $20 - 10 = 10$
   $10 + 8 = 18$
17. $5 + 8 + 4 =$ **17**
   $8 + 2 = 10$
   $5 + 2 = 7$
   $10 + 7 = 17$
18. **24 − 8 = 16; 16**
19. **3 × 7 = 21; 21**
20. **8 × 4 = 32; 32**

¹²¹⁴4	
−	8
1 6	

Unit 15: Dividing

1. (a) **20**
   (b) **4**
   (c) **5**
2. (a) **15**
   (b) **3**
   (c) **5**
3. **4**
4. **5**
5. **2**
6. **3**

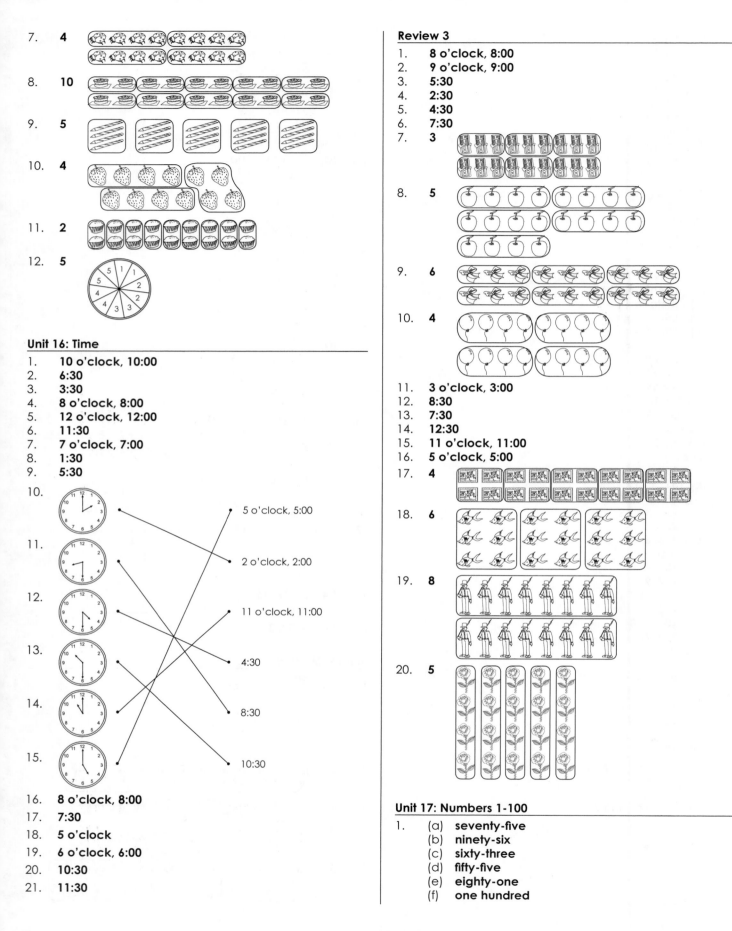

7. **4**

8. **10**

9. **5**

10. **4**

11. **2**

12. **5**

Unit 16: Time

1. **10 o'clock, 10:00**
2. **6:30**
3. **3:30**
4. **8 o'clock, 8:00**
5. **12 o'clock, 12:00**
6. **11:30**
7. **7 o'clock, 7:00**
8. **1:30**
9. **5:30**

10–15. (matching)

5 o'clock, 5:00

2 o'clock, 2:00

11 o'clock, 11:00

4:30

8:30

10:30

16. **8 o'clock, 8:00**
17. **7:30**
18. **5 o'clock**
19. **6 o'clock, 6:00**
20. **10:30**
21. **11:30**

Review 3

1. **8 o'clock, 8:00**
2. **9 o'clock, 9:00**
3. **5:30**
4. **2:30**
5. **4:30**
6. **7:30**
7. **3**

8. **5**

9. **6**

10. **4**

11. **3 o'clock, 3:00**
12. **8:30**
13. **7:30**
14. **12:30**
15. **11 o'clock, 11:00**
16. **5 o'clock, 5:00**
17. **4**

18. **6**

19. **8**

20. **5**

Unit 17: Numbers 1-100

1. (a) **seventy-five**
    (b) **ninety-six**
    (c) **sixty-three**
    (d) **fifty-five**
    (e) **eighty-one**
    (f) **one hundred**

Singapore Math Practice Level 1B

2. (a) **50**
   (b) **92**
   (c) **64**
   (d) **85**
   (e) **76**
   (f) **99**
3. **4, 5, 45**
   40, 5, 45
4. **6, 3, 63**
   60, 3, 63
5. **5, 7, 57**
   50, 7, 57
6. **7, 9, 79**
   70, 9, 79
7. **9, 0, 90**
   90, 0, 90
8. (a) 5 + 68 = **73**
   (b) 75 − 3 = **72**
   (c) 98 − 4 = **94**
   (d) 8 + 53 = **61**
   (e) 6 + 82 = **88**
   (f) 59 − 7 = **52**
   (g) 56 − 6 = **50**
9. (a) **49**
   (b) **88**
   (c) **74, 88**
   (d) **88**
   (e) **49**
10. (a) **96**
    (b) **64**
    (c) **82**
    (d) **79**
    (e) **96**
11. (a) 80, 84, **88**, **92**, 96, **100**
       84 − 80 = 4
       84 + 4 = 88
       88 + 4 = 92
       96 + 4 = 100
    (b) 66, **69**, 72, 75, **78**, **81**
       75 − 72 = 3
       66 + 3 = 69
       75 + 3 = 78
       78 + 3 = 81
    (c) **74**, **79**, 84, 89, 94
       89 − 84 = 5
       84 − 5 = 79
       79 − 5 = 74
12. (a) 42 + 4 = **46**

       40   2   2 + 4 = 6
                       40 + 6 = 46

    (b) 56 + 3 = **59**

       50   6   6 + 3 = 9
                       50 + 9 = 59

    (c) 74 + 5 = **79**

       70   4   4 + 5 = 9
                       70 + 9 = 79

    (d) 35 + 30 = **65**

       30   5   30 + 30 = 60
                       60 + 5 = 65

    (e) 68 + 20 = **88**

       60   8   60 + 20 = 80
                       80 + 8 = 88

    (f) 84 + 10 = **94**

       80   4   80 + 10 = 90
                       90 + 4 = 94

13. (a) **3, 7, 8**
       3, 15
       4, 5
       45
    (b) **4, 5, 5**
       4, 10
       5, 0
       50
    (c) **6, 3, 9**
       6, 12
       7, 2
       72
    (d) **7, 4, 13**
       7, 17
       8, 7
       87
    (e) **8, 6, 14**
       8, 20
       10, 0
       100
    (f) **5, 8, 22**
       5, 30
       8, 0
       80

14. (a)
Tens	Ones
5	3
+ 1	4
6	**7**

   (b)
Tens	Ones
7	0
+ 2	8
9	**8**

   (c)
Tens	Ones
9	1
+	6
9	**7**

   (d)
Tens	Ones
4	4
+ 3	4
7	**8**

   (e)
Tens	Ones
¹2	8
+ 6	4
9	**2**

   (f)
Tens	Ones
¹3	5
+ 4	7
8	**2**

   (g)
Tens	Ones
¹6	8
+ 1	8
8	**6**

Singapore Math Practice Level 1B

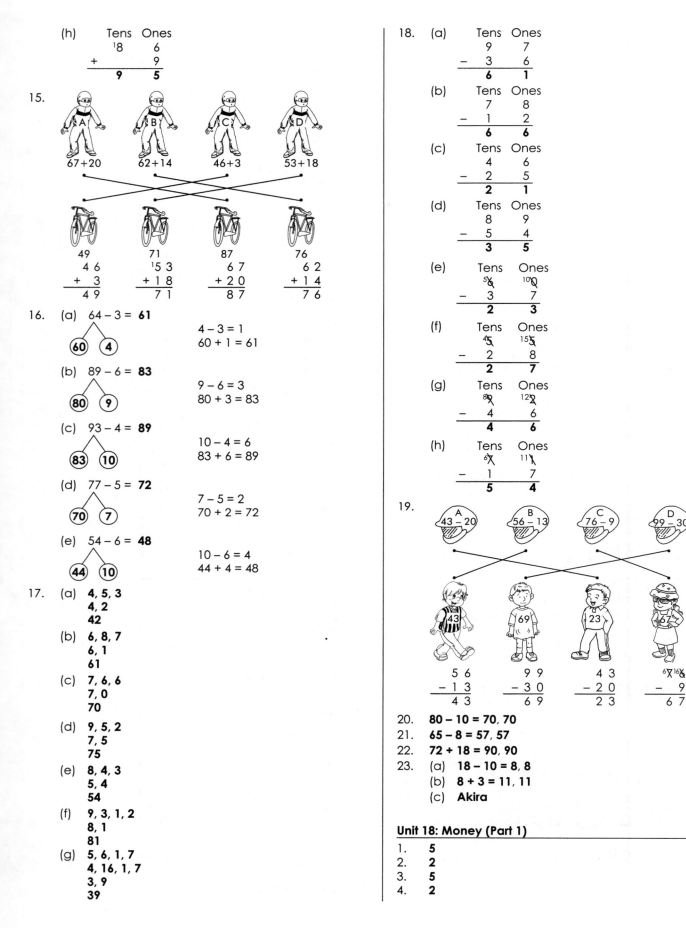

(h)
Tens	Ones
¹8	6
+	9
9	**5**

15.

A: 67+20 → 87
B: 62+14 → 76
C: 46+3 → 49
D: 53+18 → 71

49	71	87	76
4 6	¹5 3	6 7	6 2
+ 3	+1 8	+2 0	+1 4
4 9	7 1	8 7	7 6

16. (a) 64 – 3 = **61**
(60)(4)
4 – 3 = 1
60 + 1 = 61

(b) 89 – 6 = **83**
(80)(9)
9 – 6 = 3
80 + 3 = 83

(c) 93 – 4 = **89**
(83)(10)
10 – 4 = 6
83 + 6 = 89

(d) 77 – 5 = **72**
(70)(7)
7 – 5 = 2
70 + 2 = 72

(e) 54 – 6 = **48**
(44)(10)
10 – 6 = 4
44 + 4 = 48

17. (a) **4, 5, 3**
4, 2
42

(b) **6, 8, 7**
6, 1
61

(c) **7, 6, 6**
7, 0
70

(d) **9, 5, 2**
7, 5
75

(e) **8, 4, 3**
5, 4
54

(f) **9, 3, 1, 2**
8, 1
81

(g) **5, 6, 1, 7**
4, 16, 1, 7
3, 9
39

18. (a)
Tens	Ones
9	7
– 3	6
6	**1**

(b)
Tens	Ones
7	8
– 1	2
6	**6**

(c)
Tens	Ones
4	6
– 2	5
2	**1**

(d)
Tens	Ones
8	9
– 5	4
3	**5**

(e)
Tens	Ones
⁵8̶	¹⁰0̶
– 3	7
2	**3**

(f)
Tens	Ones
⁴5̶	¹⁵5̶
– 2	8
2	**7**

(g)
Tens	Ones
⁸9̶	¹²2̶
– 4	6
4	**6**

(h)
Tens	Ones
⁶7̶	¹¹1̶
– 1	7
5	**4**

19.

A: 43 – 20 → 23
B: 56 – 13 → 43
C: 76 – 9 → 67
D: 99 – 30 → 69

5 6	9 9	4 3	⁶7̶ ¹⁶6̶
– 1 3	– 3 0	– 2 0	– 9
4 3	6 9	2 3	6 7

20. **80 – 10 = 70, 70**
21. **65 – 8 = 57, 57**
22. **72 + 18 = 90, 90**
23. (a) **18 – 10 = 8, 8**
(b) **8 + 3 = 11, 11**
(c) **Akira**

Unit 18: Money (Part 1)
1. **5**
2. **2**
3. **5**
4. **2**

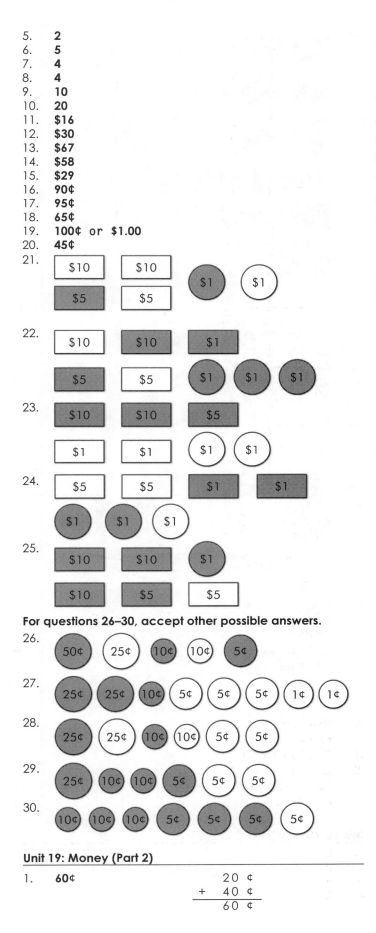

5. **2**
6. **5**
7. **4**
8. **4**
9. **10**
10. **20**
11. **$16**
12. **$30**
13. **$67**
14. **$58**
15. **$29**
16. **90¢**
17. **95¢**
18. **65¢**
19. **100¢ or $1.00**
20. **45¢**

21. | $10 | $10 | $1 | $1 |
    | $5 | $5 | | |

22. | $10 | $10 | $1 | | |
    | $5 | $5 | $1 | $1 | $1 |

23. | $10 | $10 | $5 | |
    | $1 | $1 | $1 | $1 |

24. | $5 | $5 | $1 | $1 |
    | $1 | $1 | $1 | |

25. | $10 | $10 | $1 |
    | $10 | $5 | $5 |

For questions 26–30, accept other possible answers.

26. 50¢ 25¢ 10¢ 10¢ 5¢
27. 25¢ 25¢ 10¢ 5¢ 5¢ 5¢ 1¢ 1¢
28. 25¢ 25¢ 10¢ 10¢ 5¢ 5¢
29. 25¢ 10¢ 10¢ 5¢ 5¢ 5¢
30. 10¢ 10¢ 10¢ 5¢ 5¢ 5¢ 5¢

Unit 19: Money (Part 2)

1. **60¢**

   $$\begin{array}{r} 20\ ¢ \\ +\ 40\ ¢ \\ \hline 60\ ¢ \end{array}$$

2. **95¢**

   $$\begin{array}{r} 55\ ¢ \\ +\ 40\ ¢ \\ \hline 95\ ¢ \end{array}$$

3. **35¢**

   $$\begin{array}{r} {}^{4}\cancel{5}{}^{10}\cancel{0}\ ¢ \\ -\ 1\ 5\ ¢ \\ \hline 3\ 5\ ¢ \end{array}$$

4. **110¢**

   $$\begin{array}{r} {}^{1}7\ 5\ ¢ \\ +\ 3\ 5\ ¢ \\ \hline 1\ 1\ 0\ ¢ \end{array}$$

5. **ruler** and **clip**
   65¢ + 15¢ = 80¢

6. **$22**

   $$\begin{array}{r} \$\,{}^{1}1\ 4 \\ +\ \$\ \ 8 \\ \hline \$\ 2\ 2 \end{array}$$

7. **$24**

   $$\begin{array}{r} \$\ 4\ 4 \\ -\ \$\ 2\ 0 \\ \hline \$\ 2\ 4 \end{array}$$

8. **$77**

   $$\begin{array}{r} \$\ 1\ 7 \\ +\ \$\ 6\ 0 \\ \hline \$\ 7\ 7 \end{array}$$

9. **$36**

   $$\begin{array}{r} \$\,{}^{4}\cancel{5}{}^{10}\cancel{0} \\ -\ \$\ 1\ 4 \\ \hline \$\ 3\ 6 \end{array}$$

10. **pack of playing cards** and **toy plane**
    $8 + $17 = $25

11. **$30**

    $$\begin{array}{r} \$\,{}^{1}2\ 5 \\ +\ \$\ \ 5 \\ \hline \$\ 3\ 0 \end{array}$$

12. **$8**

    $$\begin{array}{r} \$\ 3\ 8 \\ -\ \$\ 3\ 0 \\ \hline \$\ \ 8 \end{array}$$

13. **$20**

    $$\begin{array}{r} \$\,{}^{1}1\ 2 \\ +\ \$\ \ 8 \\ \hline \$\ 2\ 0 \end{array}$$

14. **$25**

    $$\begin{array}{r} \$\ 4\ 5 \\ -\ \$\ 2\ 0 \\ \hline \$\ 2\ 5 \end{array}$$

15. **skirt** and **blouse**
    $38 + $27 = $65

16. **$30**

    $$\begin{array}{r} \$\,{}^{1}2\ 5 \\ +\ \$\ \ 5 \\ \hline \$\ 3\ 0 \end{array}$$

17. **float** and **mat**
    $16 + $13 = $29

18. **$32**

    $$\begin{array}{r} \$\ 2\ 0 \\ +\ \$\ 1\ 2 \\ \hline \$\ 3\ 2 \end{array}$$

19. **$3**

    $$\begin{array}{r} \$\ 1\ 3 \\ -\ \$\ 1\ 0 \\ \hline \$\ \ 3 \end{array}$$

20. **$13**

    $$\begin{array}{r} \$\ 2\ 5 \\ -\ \$\ 1\ 2 \\ \hline \$\ 1\ 3 \end{array}$$

21. $28 + $15 = $43

    She has **$43** now.

    $$\begin{array}{r} \$\,{}^{1}2\ 8 \\ +\ \$\ 1\ 5 \\ \hline \$\ 4\ 3 \end{array}$$

Singapore Math Practice Level 1B

22. $90 – $32 = $58

$$\begin{array}{r} \$\,{}^{8}\!\!\not{9}\,{}^{10}\!\!\not{0} \\ -\ \$\ \ 3\ 2 \\ \hline \$\ \ 5\ 8 \end{array}$$

She has **$58** left.

23. 60¢ + 25¢ = 85¢

$$\begin{array}{r} 6\ 0\ ¢ \\ +\ \ 2\ 5\ ¢ \\ \hline 8\ 5\ ¢ \end{array}$$

He spends **85¢** in all.

24. 90¢ – 55¢ = 35¢

$$\begin{array}{r} {}^{8}\!\!\not{9}\,{}^{10}\!\!\not{0}\ ¢ \\ -\ \ 5\ 5\ ¢ \\ \hline 3\ 5\ ¢ \end{array}$$

He saves **35¢** every day.

25. $34 + $55 = $89

$$\begin{array}{r} \$\ 3\ 4 \\ +\ \$\ 5\ 5 \\ \hline \$\ 8\ 9 \end{array}$$

She spends **$89** altogether in a week.

Review 4

1. (a) **36**
    (b) **79**
    (c) 3 + 56 = **59**
    (d) 59 – 3 = **56**
    (e) **64**

2. 4 twenty-five-cent coins
3. 3 ten-cent coins
4. 2 ten-dollar bills
5. 5 five-dollar bills
6. 6 ten-dollar bills

$25
$1
30¢
$20
$60

7. (a)
$$\begin{array}{r} 8\ 3 \\ +\ 1\ 5 \\ \hline 9\ 8 \end{array}$$

    (b)
$$\begin{array}{r} 4\ 6 \\ +\ 1\ 2 \\ \hline 5\ 8 \end{array}$$

    (c)
$$\begin{array}{r} {}^{1}3\ 8 \\ +\ 3\ 6 \\ \hline 7\ 4 \end{array}$$

    (d)
$$\begin{array}{r} {}^{1}7\ 7 \\ +\ 2\ 3 \\ \hline 1\ 0\ 0 \end{array}$$

8. (a)
$$\begin{array}{r} 9\ 5 \\ -\ 4\ 3 \\ \hline 5\ 2 \end{array}$$

    (b)
$$\begin{array}{r} 6\ 8 \\ -\ 2\ 6 \\ \hline 4\ 2 \end{array}$$

    (c)
$$\begin{array}{r} {}^{4}\!\!\not{5}\,{}^{10}\!\!\not{0} \\ -\ 2\ 8 \\ \hline 2\ 2 \end{array}$$

    (d)
$$\begin{array}{r} {}^{7}\!\!\not{8}\,{}^{13}\!\!\not{3} \\ -\ 4\ 7 \\ \hline 3\ 6 \end{array}$$

9.

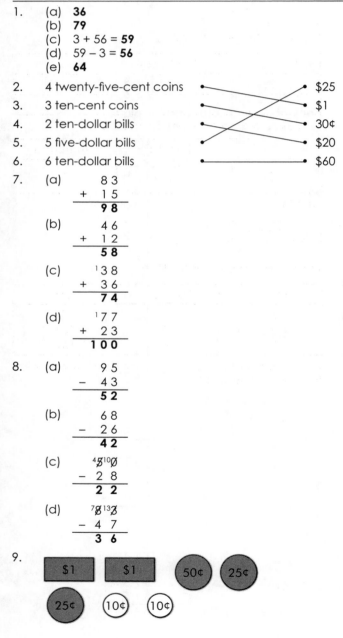

10.

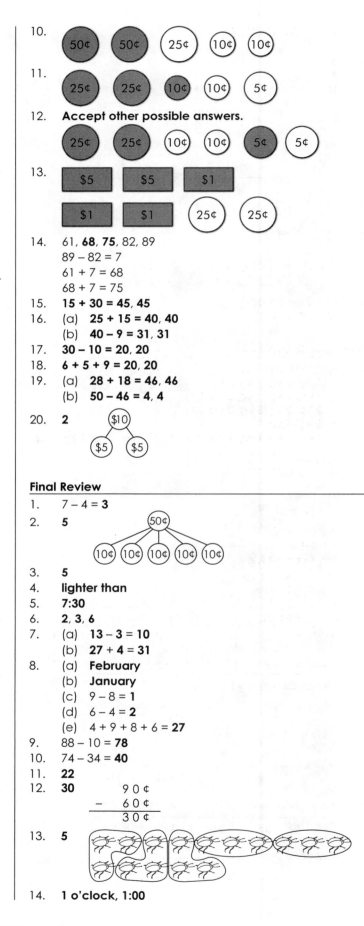

11.

12. **Accept other possible answers.**

13.

14. 61, **68**, **75**, 82, 89
    89 – 82 = 7
    61 + 7 = 68
    68 + 7 = 75

15. **15 + 30 = 45, 45**

16. (a) **25 + 15 = 40, 40**
    (b) **40 – 9 = 31, 31**

17. **30 – 10 = 20, 20**

18. **6 + 5 + 9 = 20, 20**

19. (a) **28 + 18 = 46, 46**
    (b) **50 – 46 = 4, 4**

20. **2**

Final Review

1. 7 – 4 = **3**

2. **5**

3. **5**

4. **lighter than**

5. **7:30**

6. **2, 3, 6**

7. (a) **13 – 3 = 10**
   (b) **27 + 4 = 31**

8. (a) **February**
   (b) **January**
   (c) 9 – 8 = **1**
   (d) 6 – 4 = **2**
   (e) 4 + 9 + 8 + 6 = **27**

9. 88 – 10 = **78**

10. 74 – 34 = **40**

11. **22**

12. **30**

$$\begin{array}{r} 9\ 0\ ¢ \\ -\ 6\ 0\ ¢ \\ \hline 3\ 0\ ¢ \end{array}$$

13. **5**

14. **1 o'clock, 1:00**

15. **12, 21, 36, 47, 63, 79**
16. (a) **36**
    (b) **73**
17. **8 − 3 = 5**
18.

Triangle	☆ ☆ ☆ ☆ ☆
Square	☆ ☆ ☆ ☆ ☆ ☆ ☆
Circle	☆ ☆ ☆ ☆ ☆ ☆ ☆ ☆
Oval	☆ ☆ ☆

19. **7, 8, 78**
20. **75 − 45 = 30, 30**
21. **5 × 2 = 10, 10**
22. **4 + 18 = 22, 22**
23. **5**

24. **62 − 22 = 40, 40**
25. **50 − 38 = 12, 12**

Challenge Questions

1. The five ways are:
   - **1 kg, 2 kg, 2 kg, 5 kg**
   - **1 kg, 1 kg, 1 kg, 2 kg, 5 kg**
   - **2 kg, 2 kg, 2 kg, 2 kg, 2 kg**
   - **5 kg, 5 kg**
   - **1 kg, 1 kg, 1 kg, 1 kg, 1 kg, 1 kg, 1 kg, 1 kg, 1 kg, 1 kg**

2.

1st digit	?	3
2nd digit	?	

  } 9

   9 − 3 = 6
   3 + 3 = 6
   The second digit is 3.
   3 + 3 = 6
   The first digit is 6.
   The number is **63**.

3. A bird has 2 legs. A cat has 4 legs.

Birds	Cats	Total
1 × 2 = 2	2 × 4 = 8	2 + 8 = 10
2 × 2 = 4	3 × 4 = 12	4 + 12 = 16
3 × 2 = 6	4 × 4 = 16	6 + 16 = 22

   He has **3** birds and **4** cats.

4. Clock A

   10 min

   | 2 | 2 | 2 | 2 | 2 |
   ① ② ③ ④ ⑤

   Clock B

   10 min

   | 5 | 5 |
   ① ②

   5 + 2 = 7
   The two clocks will chime **7** times in 10 minutes.

5.

$1	$5	$10	$20	Total
✓		✓	✓	$31
✓	✓		✓	$26
	✓	✓	✓	$35

She has **1 five-dollar bill**, **1 ten-dollar bill**, and **1 twenty-dollar bill**.

6.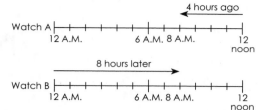

   The actual time is **8 A.M.**

7. 5 + 5 + 5 + 5 = 20
   Therefore, the value of ▲ is **5**.
   ♥ + ♥ + ♥ + 5 + 5 = 16
   ♥ + ♥ + ♥ + 10 = 16
   ♥ + ♥ + ♥ = 16 − 10
   = 6
   2 + 2 + 2 = 6
   Therefore, the value of ♥ is **2**.

8.

Left page	Right page	Sum
28	29	57
30	31	61

   Kenji was looking at **pages 30** and **31**.

9.

1st digit	2nd digit	Difference
2	7	5
2	9	7

   I am **29**.

10.

   1 hour   5 hours

   4 P.M.   9 P.M.

   The cartoon started at **3 P.M.**

11.

1st coin	2nd coin	Sum
50	50	$1
25	50	75¢
10	50	60¢

The greatest amount of money that Elian could receive from his mother was **75¢**.

Notes

Singapore Math Practice Level 1B

Fill in each blank with the correct answer. Each ▦ stands for 1 unit.

18.

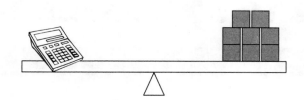

The mass of the calculator is _____ units.

19.

The mass of the present is _____ units.

20.

The mass of the apple is _____ units.

Unit 12 : NUMBERS 1–40

Examples:

1. 5 and 20 make **25**.

3. 29 + 2 = **31**

Tens	Ones
¹2	9
+	2
3	1

2. **38** is 2 less than 40.

4. 38 – 19 = **19**

Tens	Ones
²3	¹8
– 1	9
1	9

Circle groups of 10 in each set of pictures. Count the items, and write the correct answers on the lines.

1.

_____

4.

_____

2.

_____

5.

_____

3.

_____

6. Write the following numbers in words.

(a) 20 _____

(b) 15 _____

(c) 39 _____

(d) 27 _____

(e) 11 _____

(f) 40 _____

(g) 35 _____

(h) 21 _____

7. Write the correct numbers on the lines provided.

(a) fourteen _____   (e) twenty-six _____

(b) twenty-four _____   (f) eighteen _____

(c) thirty _____   (g) thirty-two _____

(d) nineteen _____   (h) thirteen _____

3. Fill in each blank with the correct answer.

(a) 30 and 6 make _____.   (e) 30 and 3 make _____.

(b) 20 and 1 make _____.   (f) 10 and 4 make _____.

(c) 10 and 7 make _____.   (g) 20 and 6 make _____.

(d) 20 and 8 make _____.   (h) 30 and 9 make _____.

Singapore Math Practice Level 1B

Fill in each blank with the correct answer.

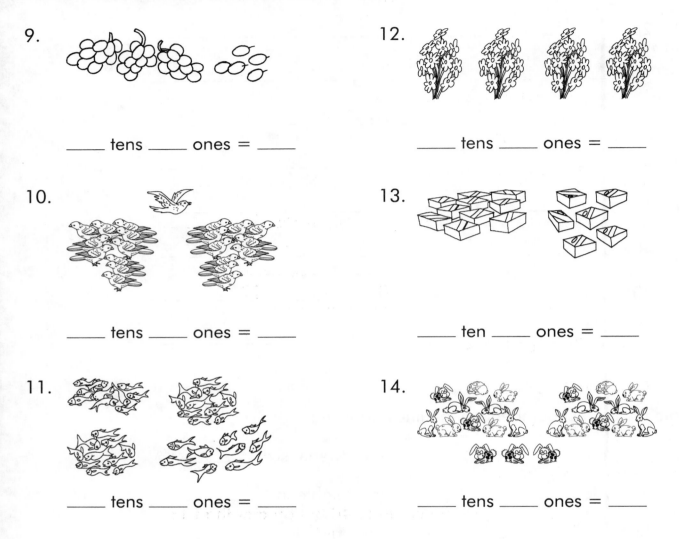

9. _____ tens _____ ones = _____

10. _____ tens _____ ones = _____

11. _____ tens _____ ones = _____

12. _____ tens _____ ones = _____

13. _____ ten _____ ones = _____

14. _____ tens _____ ones = _____

Fill in each blank with the correct answer.

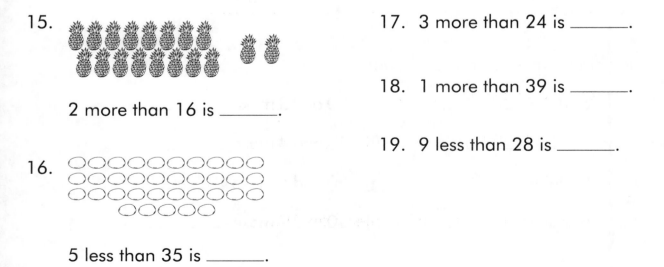

15. 2 more than 16 is _____.

16. 5 less than 35 is _____.

17. 3 more than 24 is _____.

18. 1 more than 39 is _____.

19. 9 less than 28 is _____.

Singapore Math Practice Level 1

| 35 | 22 | 28 | 17 |

(a) The largest number is _____.

(b) The smallest number is _____.

(c) _____ is greater than 28.

(d) _____ is smaller than 22.

(e) 28 is greater than _____ and _____ but smaller than _____.

1. | 16 | 31 | 40 | 27 |

(a) The smallest number is _____.

(b) The largest number is _____.

(c) 2 more than 29 is _____.

(d) 2 less than 29 is _____.

(e) _____ and _____ are smaller than 40 but greater than 16.

2. | 19 | 40 | 21 | 35 |

(a) The largest number is _____.

(b) The smallest number is _____.

(c) _____ is 2 more than 19.

(d) _____ is 5 less than 40.

(e) _____ is smaller than 35 but greater than 19.

23. | 28 | 14 | 17 | 31 | 25 |

(a) The smallest number is _____.

(b) The largest number is _____.

(c) _____ is 3 more than 28.

(d) _____ is 3 less than 17.

(e) _____ is greater than 17 but smaller than 28.

Match the problems on the left to the answers on the right.

24. 2 less than 21   •   •   38

25. 1 more than 37   •   •   24

26. 3 more than 20   •   •   19

27. 2 more than 23   •   •   15

28. 3 less than 18   •   •   23

29. 1 less than 25   •   •   25

Complete the number patterns.

30. _____, 14, _____, 20, 23

31. 9, 14, 19, _____, _____

32. 25, _____, 35, _____, 45

33. 28, _____, 32, 34, _____

34. 18, 24, 30, _____, _____

Singapore Math Practice Level 1B